The Colorful Expressions of Your Soul

A Mandala Coloring Book and Meditative Creative Journal

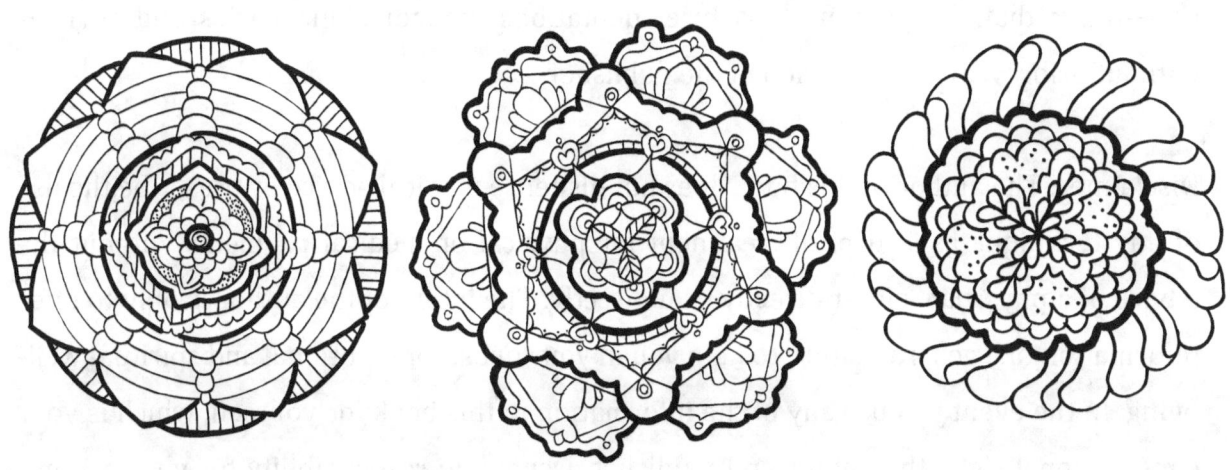

Crystal Simpelo

ISBN: 978-1-940847-31-3
LCCN: 2014905978

Printed in the United States of America

DEDICATIONS

This book is dedicated to the bright and loving memory of my grandparents.

Lola Pilar, thank you for taking care of my siblings and me. Thank you for your love and support. Thank you for your wonderful cooking and joyful laughter.

Lolo Ato, thank you for supporting me in my musical ambitions. Thank you for applauding my piano playing, even today.

Lola Goyang and Lolo Ciano, although we have only met once, thank you for my memorable visit to the Philippines. You taught me to appreciate the little things in life.

RAVING REVIEWS

"Such A Treat For My Creative Inner Child!"

"Crystal Simpelo does a fantastic job anticipating exactly what you'll need to express *The Colorful Expressions of Your Soul*. Her mandala coloring book is packed with beautifully hand drawn works of art and was such a treat for my creative inner child. This was a clearly thought out product made with love and I loved every bit of it." --Lena Anani, Author of *OMG Do It Now: Be the Voice You Want to Hear in the World*

"Led Me To A Understanding About Meditation And Chakras!"

"Crystal Simpelo shares her struggles that she has gone through with art, teaching us that anybody can be creative. *The Colorful Expressions of Your Soul* has led me to an understanding about meditation and chakras. It is a wonderful guide for anyone interested in learning more about chakras and how to balance them in an artistic way. Simpelo's concept on combining art with meditation is brilliant, teaching us different techniques to help clear our chakras, and center ourselves to become balanced with the world." --Katie Van Eynde, Author of *Motivate Your Magnetic Mind*, KatieLovesLife.com

"Better Understanding To Reach The Upper Plateaus of Peace And Happiness!"

"Crystal Simpelo's fascinating book shows how we can use art in more ways than just as a medium to express ourselves. Harnessing your inner energies and aligning your Chakras to become an enlightened human being has never been so informative and beautiful. I have learned through Simpelo's experiences as she spoke to me from within the pages of this book. After reading her most recent achievement, I too now have a better understanding on how to reach the upper plateaus of peace and happiness." --Anne O'Brien, Special Needs Professional

"Artwork Was A Nice Form Of Therapy!"

"This book is eye opening and very calming. Using the body parts and incorporating them into the artwork was a nice form of therapy. Using the mandalas to color while opening your mind was an interesting concept. I also really liked that it was both reading and coloring. I think you did a great job with the artwork as well! Different designs that will turn out great for each person who chooses to take part!" --Jan Gilman, Homemaker

"A Very Inspiring Read As Well As Absolutely Stunning Art!"

"*The Colorful Expressions of Your Soul: A Mandala Coloring Book and Meditative Creative Journal* by Crystal Simpelo, is an amazing and insightful look at human emotions and how one can use their artistic talents to create a positive outlook on life. Beautifully written and put together with absolutely stunning art, this book really gives the reader an understanding of the different Chakra points and the importance of them all. Simpelo is a very talented writer as well as artist and through her words it's easy to see just how passionate she is when it comes to her art. A very inspiring read as well as absolutely stunning art that really relaxes you and puts your soul at ease. I highly recommend this book for any artist, no matter what your craft may be, as well as anybody else looking to improve their outlook on life." --Adam Janis, Adjustment Clerk

"Inspiration To Start That Lifestyle Change!"

"The book, *The Colorful Expressions of Your Soul: A Mandala Coloring Book and Meditative Creative Journal*, by Crystal Simpelo explains different ways to balance your seven main chakras to live a more positive life. This short piece not only provides information on how to become an overall better person, but also includes coloring of mandalas and space for reflective writing. Reading the author's advice and personal anecdotes alone provides inspiration in wanting to start that lifestyle change. After reading this book, I feel I have many different tools to use to help rid any negativity in life and to live my life to its fullest potential. This unique book is a great read for anyone looking for self-improvement!" --Kristine Perry, Doctor of Pharmacy

"True Nourishment For The Mind, Body, Heart And Soul!"

"Positive, uplifting, creative, and refreshing! A true nourishment for the mind, body, heart, and soul. A map to balance ourselves; our lives is depicted beautifully within Simpelo's words. She has created a clear guide and understanding of how we can enhance our life and relationships through the experience of creating art and positive thinking." --Michelle Melendez, K-5 Art Teacher

"A Wonderful Approach To Art And Meditation!"

"What a wonderful approach to art and meditation! As a father and lawyer, stressors abound. The coloring, however, was so calming and allowed time to focus inward- to breath and relax!" --Charles R. Kiser, Attorney

"The Mandalas Are Beautiful!"

"This book is wonderful! The mandalas are beautiful! Such creativity all around and a positive look on life! I really enjoyed learning about the different Chakras. This book is great for me especially because I get stressed out so easily." --Christina Simpelo, Registered Nurse

CONTENTS

Acknowledgements..1

Introduction...3

Shine Bright Like a Ruby..5

     Abundance...7

     Believe...11

     Grounded..15

Release Your Inner Wild Child..19

     Create...23

     Friendship..27

     Happiness...31

If It Makes You Happy...35

     Confidence..37

     Motivation..41

     Strength...45

Spread the Delicious Love...49

     Value..51

     Love...55

     Embrace...59

Sing It Like a Rock Star..63

     Dream...65

     Truth..69

     Communication...73

Do Your Crazy Dance...77

     Imagine..79

     Smile..83

     Dance...87

Are You Even Listening?..91

     Enlightenment...95

     Awakening..99

     Intuition...103

Time to Embark on Your Journey...107

Frequently Asked Questions..109

Final Thoughts..113

About the Author...115

FREE Chakra Poster...117

ACKNOWLEDGEMENTS

I want to thank my parents, Melanio and Fortune Simpelo, and my siblings Chris and Christina Simpelo for their endless love and support in everything I do. You have all taught, encouraged, and believed in me.

Thank you to my loving hubby and best friend, Drew Gilman, for showing continuous love, support, and encouragement in all that I do. Having your there by my side is a huge component in reaching my goals.

Thank you Lena Anani for helping me write, edit, and create this book. You are a wonderful mentor, coach, teacher, author, and friend. I cannot put into words how much your guidance means to me.

Thank you to all my awesome massage clients. Without you, I would not be able to love my job as much as I do.

Thank you to my family, friends, colleagues, teachers, and students. You have all been brought into my life for a reason. Your advice, encouragement, and support are greatly appreciated. You rock!

INTRODUCTION

"Life isn't about finding yourself. Life is about creating yourself."
-G.B. Shaw

Have you had moments where your thoughts are constantly running on overdrive and you cannot keep up with them? Have you been trapped in a funk lately and cannot seem to make it any better? Have you been feeling like your life has been going in an uncontrollable downward spiral of negative events? Feeling unmotivated? Feeling drained physically and emotionally? This may be the book to help you free yourself from these feelings.

My name is Crystal Simpelo and at an early age, I could not wait for art class. It was without a doubt my favorite subject. I continued to experiment with different types of art throughout high school, and soon found that I enjoyed art of all forms. I was in love!

After high school, I knew I wanted to continue creating so I applied for the Time Arts program at Northern Illinois University and received my Bachelor's degree in Fine Arts. I was sure I would land a job after graduating. I did….just not using my artistic abilities. After a couple years of feeling frustrated and discouraged, I asked myself over and over, "Was I not a good enough artist?"

It was while I was watercolor painting a piece for my mother when I realized (palm-slap to forehead), I have learned so much about myself and my artistic style through my experience with art. Creating art made me feel awesome, and even though I was not creating for a living, I had no regrets.

Still working my full time office job, I wanted to do something more rewarding, so in 2010 I attended Cortiva Institute to become a Licensed Massage Therapist. Currently, I work as a Legal Assistant, Licensed Massage Therapist, a Freelance Graphic Designer, and a Meditative Art Teacher. I love what I do!

Meditation and Art have always been an integral part of my life. I have been practicing meditative art for the past ten years. I teach art workshops where I guide others in creating art on their own as a meditative tool they can use in their daily lives. I show others how to fall in love with art like I did. I also practice chakra balancing and meditation with my massage clients.

While teaching one of my art classes, I saw how much everybody was gaining in creating their art pieces. It was a fun therapy session where they could let their inner child come out and let go of any worries. That was the moment when I knew I wanted to share my meditative tools with more people.

Recently, my heart led me to create this meditative art book, because I love knowing that my fun tools/visualizations have such a positive impact on my life. I felt called to share my love for meditative art with you, so you can feel the same way! Simply knowing that others can benefit from visualizing and coloring my Mandalas is an awesome feeling.

By implementing my meditative art tools, you can change your life. You can be creative and positive. You can learn how to balance your chakras by letting yourself shine, releasing your inner child, being one with nature, taking care of yourself, singing, dancing, and using positive affirmations. You can heal yourself physically, emotionally, and spiritually in doing these things. You will be able to feel grounded, creative, confident, and loving. You will experience positive self-expression, intuition, and joy for life. Sounds pretty awesome right? Each chapter will give examples on how to balance your seven main Chakras. Keep reading and enjoy your journey!

SHINE BRIGHT LIKE A RUBY

"Meditate daily, and soon your inner
strength and mind power will grow."
- Remez Sasson

The Root Chakra is located at the base of the spine and is associated with the color red. This Chakra is the center of grounding and foundation. When you have a balanced Root Chakra, you will experience feelings of security, reach financial independence, become grounded, and a gain a sense of stability. If you have an overactive Root Chakra you may experience feelings of greed and have materialistic tendencies. If you have a Root Chakra that isn't active, or isn't active enough, you may experience resistance to change, nervousness, and fear.

It is important to know about the Root Chakra. Financial stability is a huge part of our everyday lives. Raising a family, paying our bills, and working, are just some of the key factors that may cause an imbalance in your Root Chakra. These negative feelings will absorb into your Root Chakra which will cause this energy center to become blocked. It is important to balance this chakra to feel grounded.

All of our chakras are working with one another. When any of your Chakras are imbalanced, it may cause others to be as well. We want all of our Chakras to be balanced with one another to experience a natural flow in all our Chakras. In this clearing process, the root chakra is the first one on the list that needs to be addressed. Located at the base of the spine, the Root Chakra is the main Chakra that will allow us to be grounded and gain a sense of stability.

There are many things I do to balance my Root Chakra. One of my personal favorite methods is meditation. By doing so, I focus on bringing white light into my Root Chakra center. I sit or lie comfortably and imagine a beam of light coming down and filling this

Chakra and removing all negative energy out. I close my eyes and breathe deeply while focusing at the base of my spine.

When I balance my Root Chakra by meditating and imagining a bright light, I can feel a pulsing sensation at that Chakra. With focus and practice you can feel this sensation as well. I believe that everyone perceives their Chakras differently. To me, they look like colorful spinning spheres and when they are balanced, I can see all the colors of each Chakra bright and clear. I practice meditation on my chakras even when I am giving a massage. I am able to focus on each one and also do the same on my clients. After my massage treatments, I feel refreshed, recharged, and grounded.

I have known some that meditate to their Chakra before going to bed. This too is a good technique that may work for you. These people are able to forget about and release the negativity that took place throughout the day and "press the reset button" when approaching the following day. They are able to push everything past them, and focus on the next day being amazing!

If you apply this tool of meditation into your Root Chakra, you may notice that you now have more motivation to achieve your goals. You may gain control of things in your life and feel grounded and stabile. You may feel committed, strong, centered, and more energetic.

In the following coloring pages, pick a Mandala that you are attracted to at this moment. Take a few minutes before creating it to meditate into your Root Chakra. Focus on a bright white light at the base of your spine and visualize this Chakra turning a beautiful bright red. As you color in your Mandala, continue to focus on your Root Chakra and let all the worries that occupy your mind disappear. When you feel you have completed your Mandala, take time to journal about what you experienced before, during, and after coloring this particular Mandala.

Balance your Root Chakra by allowing it to shine as bright as the sun so you can feel committed, strong, grounded, and energetic.

Abundance

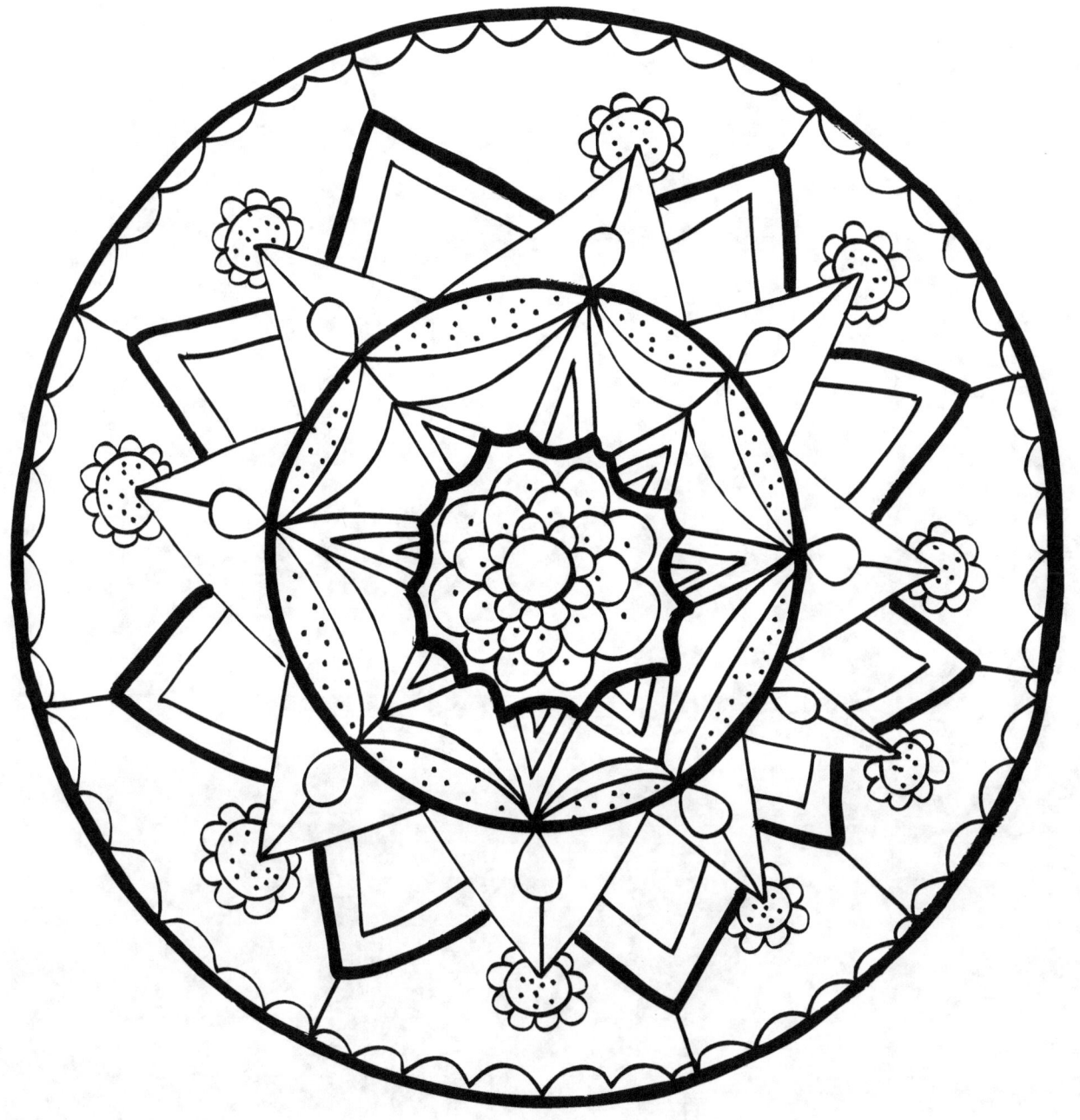

I visualize myself in abundant wealth.

Date:_____

Journal about it...

_____
_____
_____
_____
_____
_____
_____
_____
_____
_____
_____
_____
_____
_____
_____
_____
_____
_____

Believe

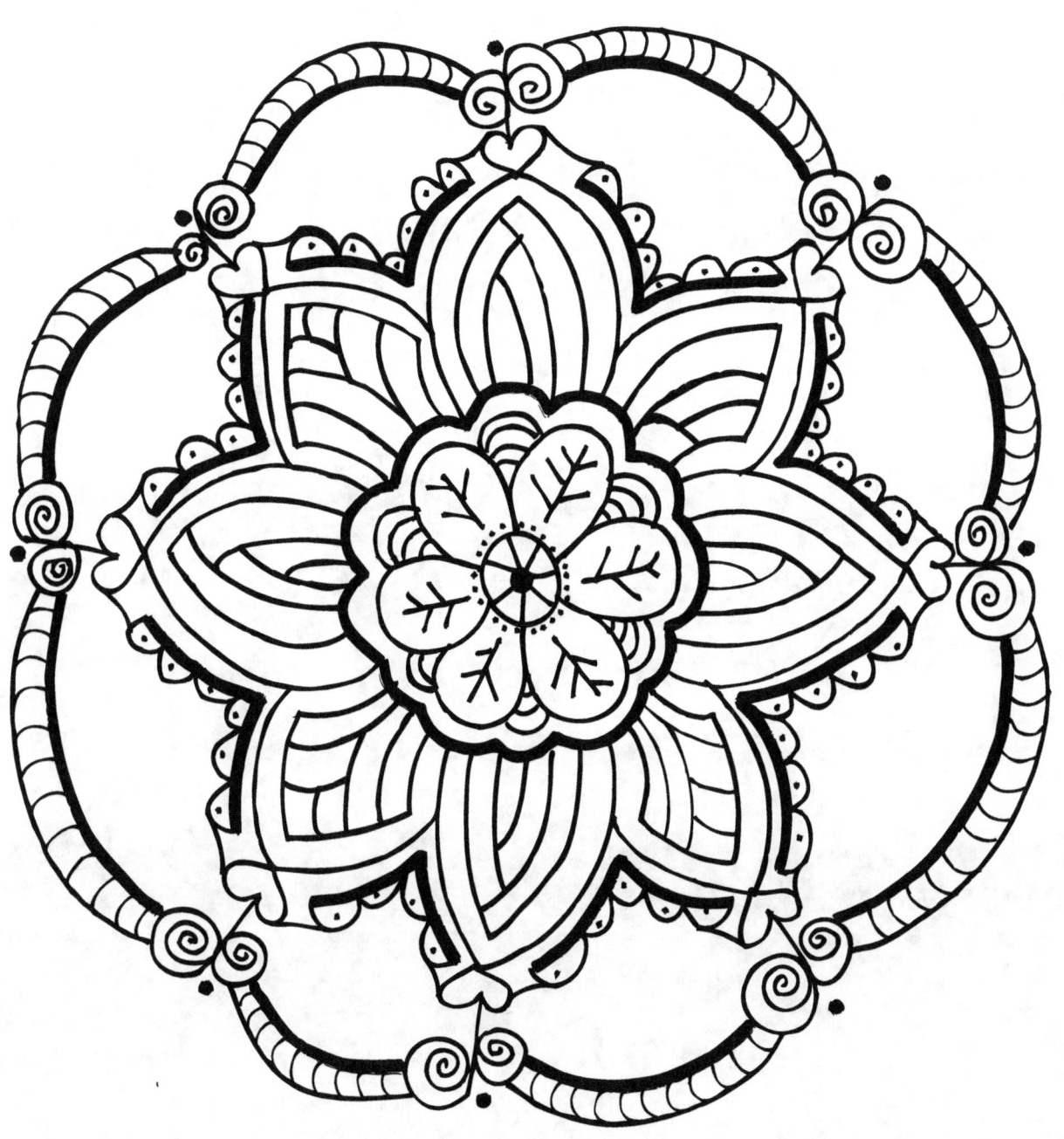

I always find a way to succeed.

Date:_____

Journal about it...

_____
_____
_____
_____
_____
_____
_____
_____
_____
_____
_____
_____
_____
_____
_____
_____
_____
_____
_____

Grounded

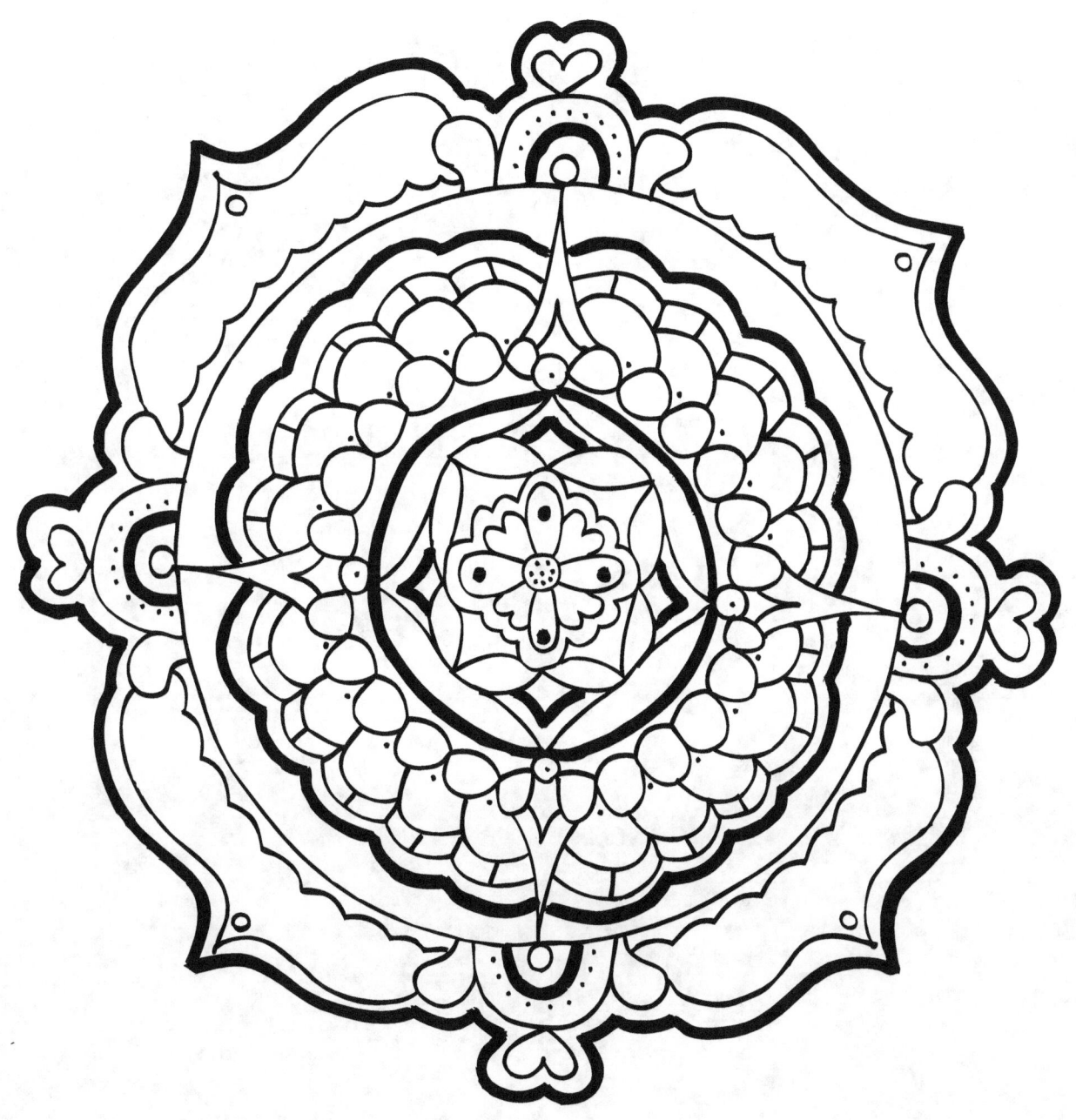

I am protected, secure, and safe.

Date:_____

Journal about it...

_____

_____

_____

_____

_____

_____

_____

_____

_____

_____

_____

_____

_____

_____

_____

_____

RELEASE YOUR INNER WILD CHILD

*"If you hear a voice within you say 'You cannot paint,'
then by all means paint and that voice will be silenced."*
-Vincent Van Gogh

The Sacral Chakra is located at the lower abdomen, about two inches below the navel and two inches in. It is associated with the color orange. This Chakra is the center of creativity, pleasure, and relationships. When you have a balanced Sacral Chakra you will experience free flowing creativity and have healthy relationships. If you have an overactive Chakra you may experience over-emotional tendencies and be overly attached in your relationships. If you have a Sacral Chakra that isn't active, or isn't active enough, you may experience a lack of motivation and disconnect towards others.

It is important to know about the Sacral Chakra. It is obvious that we all love doing things that make us feel good, many of which are in the company of our friends and family. Stressors from work and relationships with others may cause you to have an imbalanced Sacral Chakra. These stressors will also cause you to lack motivation to create, which will then cloud the Sacral Chakra even more. These negative stressors will absorb into your Sacral Chakra, causing this energy center to be blocked. It is necessary to balance your Sacral Chakra in order to experience a happy life with free flowing creativity and maintain healthy relationships.

The Sacral Chakra is the second Chakra that needs to be addressed. Our relationships with others can have a huge impact on our energy, whether it be good or bad energy. Bad energy can cloud our Sacral Chakra in layers, which might take a lot of time to clear up. Being aware of these negative energies and allowing yourself to recognize them and shift your attitude in a more positive way is a great start to begin your clearing process. Clearing this Chakra will allow you to feel motivated, be creative, and have healthy interactions with others.

I balance my Sacral Chakra by inviting others to create with me. I host frequent art gatherings to create art with others in hope of lifting our vibrations. Being in good company while doing things you love is a phenomenal way to balance your Chakras. This is a great way to incorporate creativity with positive socialization. Sharing these moments will bring you even closer to those you love.

In every group meeting, I teach others how to incorporate art as a healing tool in their lives. Teaching and creating with others makes me feel good, and makes my students feel good. I love witnessing everyone's process of creation and seeing their end result. Each person has their own person journey and growth in this process. Since the Sacral Chakra is the center for creativity, pleasure, and relationships, inviting others to create art with me allows my Sacral Chakra to be balanced in all these arenas.

When a friend of mine told me she wished she could create art, I informed her that she could turn that wish into a reality. After meditating with others and learning how to paint and draw, she was able use meditative art to lift her vibration and be creative. She was able to open up her Sacral Chakra and let her inner child come out.

If you decide to be creative with others, you will feel more creative and gain inspiration. A good start might be to start your own art community to share your art with others, or organize a group art project to create with friends. You might find your newfound ability of accepting and embracing new experiences easier when your Sacral Chakra is balanced. You may also notice that in doing so, you attract new healthy relationships as well.

In the following coloring pages, pick a Mandala that you find attractive at this moment. Invite someone to join you in creating this Mandala, or any form of art. Take a few minutes before creating it to meditate into your Sacral Chakra. Focus a bright white light at your lower abdomen, about two inches below the navel and two inches in and visualize this Chakra turning into a beautiful bright orange. As you color in your Mandala, continue to focus on your Sacral Chakra. If you are unable to color this Mandala with the company of others, visualize yourself sitting at a round table with all the people you love. Imagine yourself sitting with your parents, grandparents, kids, siblings, friends, aunts, uncles, and even those who have passed. Everyone is laughing and admiring all the beautiful work that you are all creating. When you feel your Mandala is completed, take time to journal about what you experienced before, during, and after coloring this particular Mandala.

Balance your Sacral Chakra by releasing your inner child and be creative with others to form healthy relationships.

The Colorful Expressions of Your Soul by Crystal Simpelo

Create

I have free flowing creativity.

Date:_____

Journal about it...

_____

_____

_____

_____

_____

_____

_____

_____

_____

_____

_____

_____

_____

_____

_____

_____

_____

Friendship

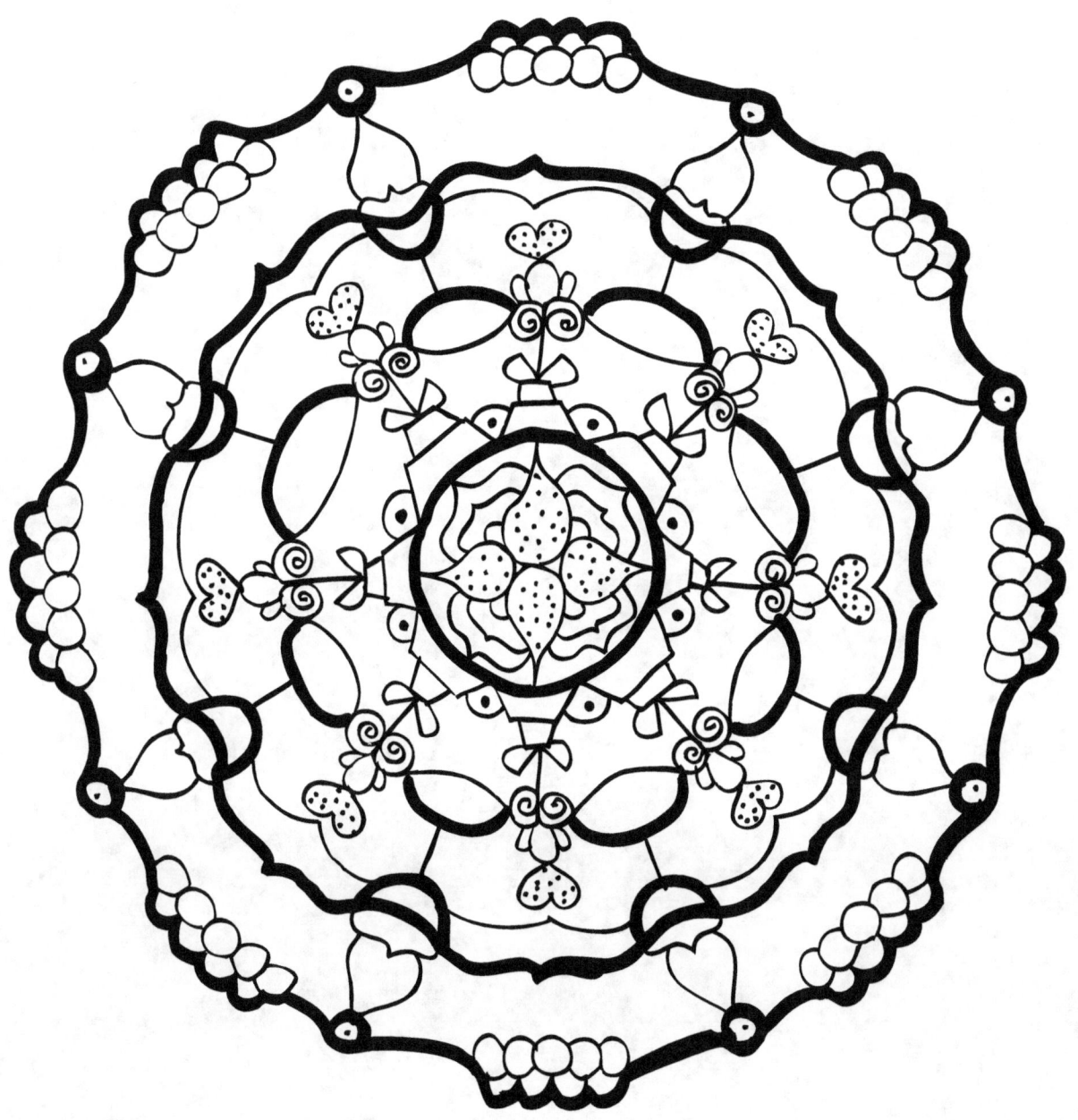

My life is filled with loving relationships.

Date:_____

Journal about it...

_____

_____

_____

_____

_____

_____

_____

_____

_____

_____

_____

_____

_____

_____

_____

_____

_____

_____

Happiness

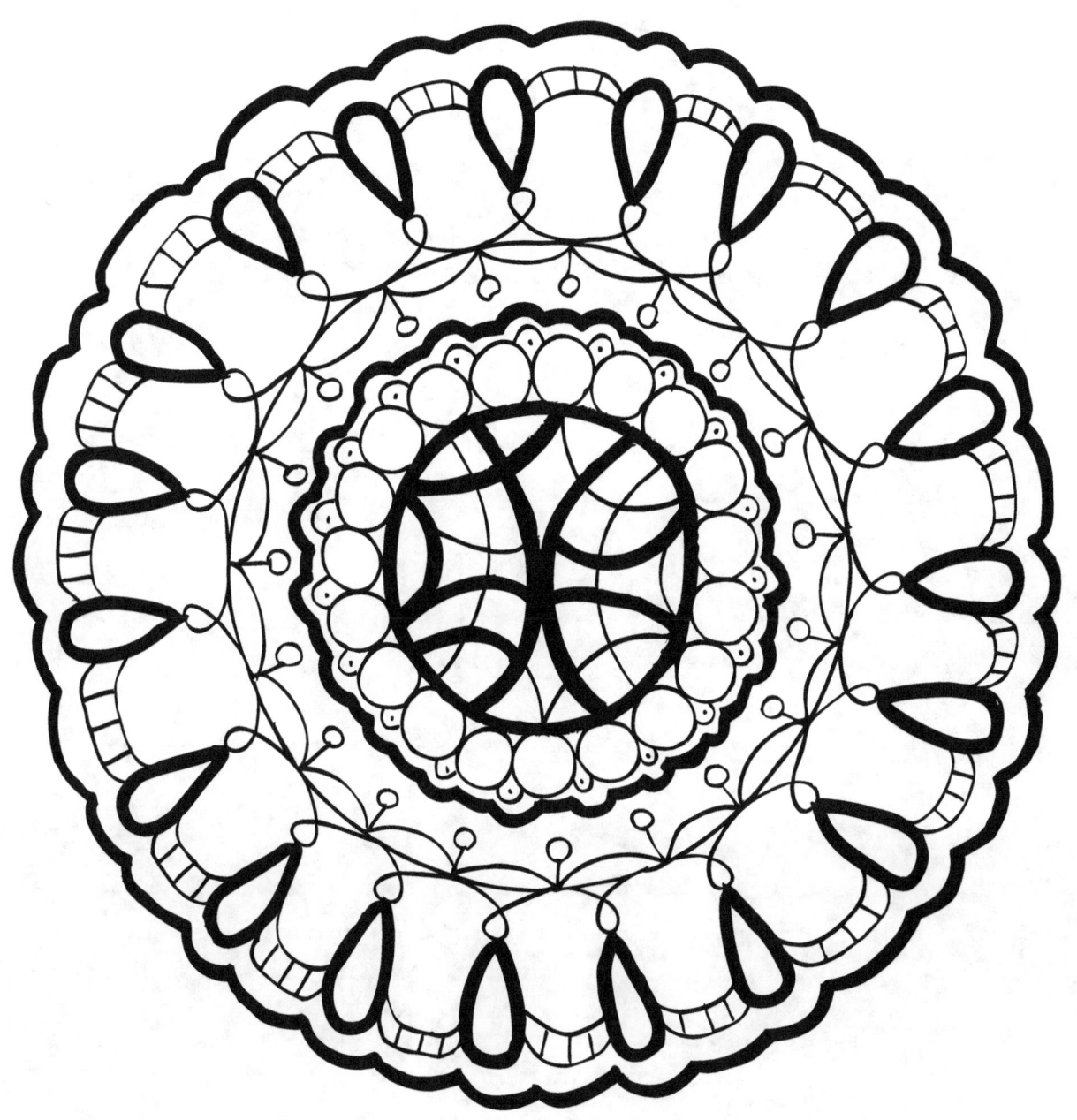

I am supported and
encouraged to follow my passion.

Date:_____

Journal about it...

_____
_____
_____
_____
_____
_____
_____
_____
_____
_____
_____
_____
_____
_____
_____
_____
_____
_____
_____

IF IT MAKES YOU HAPPY

"Our task must be to free ourselves...
by widening our circle of compassion to embrace all living
creatures and the whole of nature and its beauty."
- Albert Einstein

The Solar Plexus Chakra is located in the upper abdomen in between the navel and chest, and is associated with the color yellow. This Chakra is the center of motivation, desire, and self-worth. When you have a balanced Solar Plexus Chakra you will have self-confidence, be better equipped to achieve your goals, and have a strong sense of motivation towards your desires. Those who have an overactive Solar Plexus Chakra tend to be perfectionists or may have tendencies of being judgmental or overly critical of others. Those who have an inactive or low active Solar Plexus Chakra tend to be indecisive or timid people who may experience mental blocks often.

It is important to know about the Solar Plexus Chakra. Life is full of choices. Sometimes we feel that certain decisions may not be the right choice or that we do not deserve certain things because of how we feel about ourselves. Decision making is a common stressor in our lives. These negative feelings about yourself will absorb into your Solar Plexus Chakra causing this energy center to be blocked. It is important to balance your Solar Plexus in order to maintain motivation to accomplish your desires and find your value in life.

The Solar Plexus Chakra is the third Chakra that needs to be addressed. When Chakras have built up negative energy it can affect our bodies physically as well. The Solar Plexus Chakra deals with our motivation, desires, and self-worth. If we are not feeling good about ourselves it transfers over and has a negative effect on our choices which will cloud any sense of motivation towards what we desire. If we believe in what we are worth, then everything will fall into place in a positive way. Clearing this Chakra will allow you to be motivated in achieving your goals and make you feel great about yourself!

I like to be one with nature to balance my Solar Plexus Chakra. I enjoy running outside or looking up at the stars. I love having a nice meal outdoors to admire the beautiful scenery. I have some of the best meditations when I go camping. I sit by the campfire, listen to the crackling of the firewood, and enjoy being in the moment. I enjoy the little things. I pay attention to the trees, flowers, fire and sun. I am able to forget about the things in life that may cause stress and allow myself to meditate and feel good about myself.

I know others who enjoy running outside without the use of ear buds and music to help them focus. They pay attention on what is going on around them and become one with nature. Running in itself is a form of meditation and one can feel connected with nature while running and paying attention to their breathing and their surroundings.

If you decide to let yourself become one with nature to balance your Solar Plexus Chakra you may feel stronger and more confident.

In the following coloring pages, pick a Mandala that you are attracted to at this moment. Complete this Mandala outdoors. If you are unable to be outdoors, close your eyes for a moment and visualize yourself outdoors at your favorite place. This can be any place that makes you happy, even if it is somewhere you have never been. It can also be a place you have created in your own mind to be perfect. You have all creative power when it comes to what you do with your mind. Take a few minutes before getting to your special place to meditate into your Solar Plexus Chakra and really feel that happiness. Focus a bright white light at your upper abdomen in between your navel and chest. Visualize this Chakra turning a beautiful bright yellow. As you color in your Mandala, continue to focus on your Solar Plexus Chakra. When you feel you have completed your Mandala, take time to journal about what you experienced before, during, and after coloring this particular Mandala.

Balance your Solar Plexus Chakra by visualizing yourself at your happy place in nature to feel strong, confident, and energetic.

The Colorful Expressions of Your Soul by Crystal Simpelo

Confidence

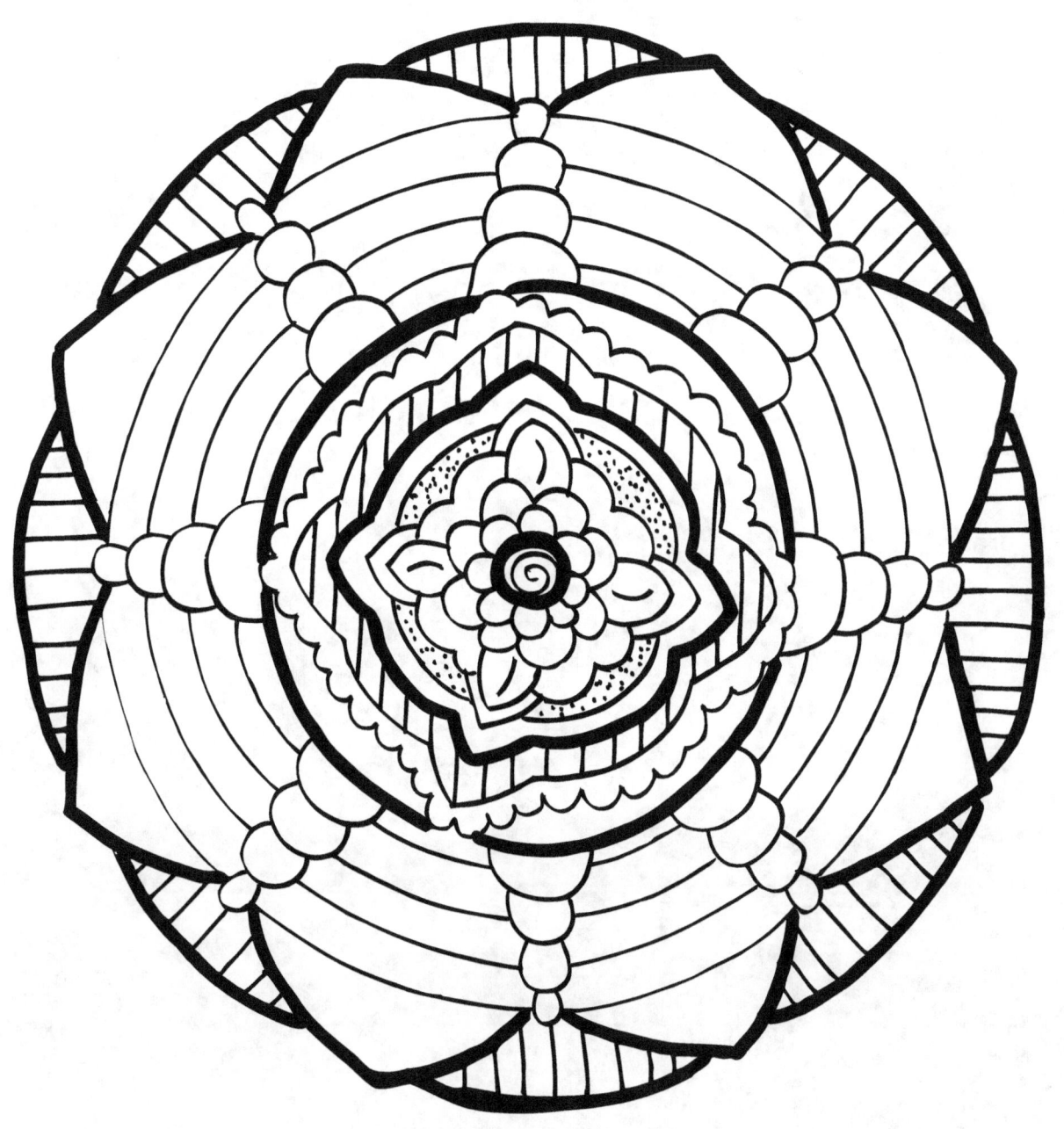

I love and trust in my creative gifts.

Date:_____

Journal about it...

_____

_____

_____

_____

_____

_____

_____

_____

_____

_____

_____

_____

_____

_____

_____

_____

Motivation

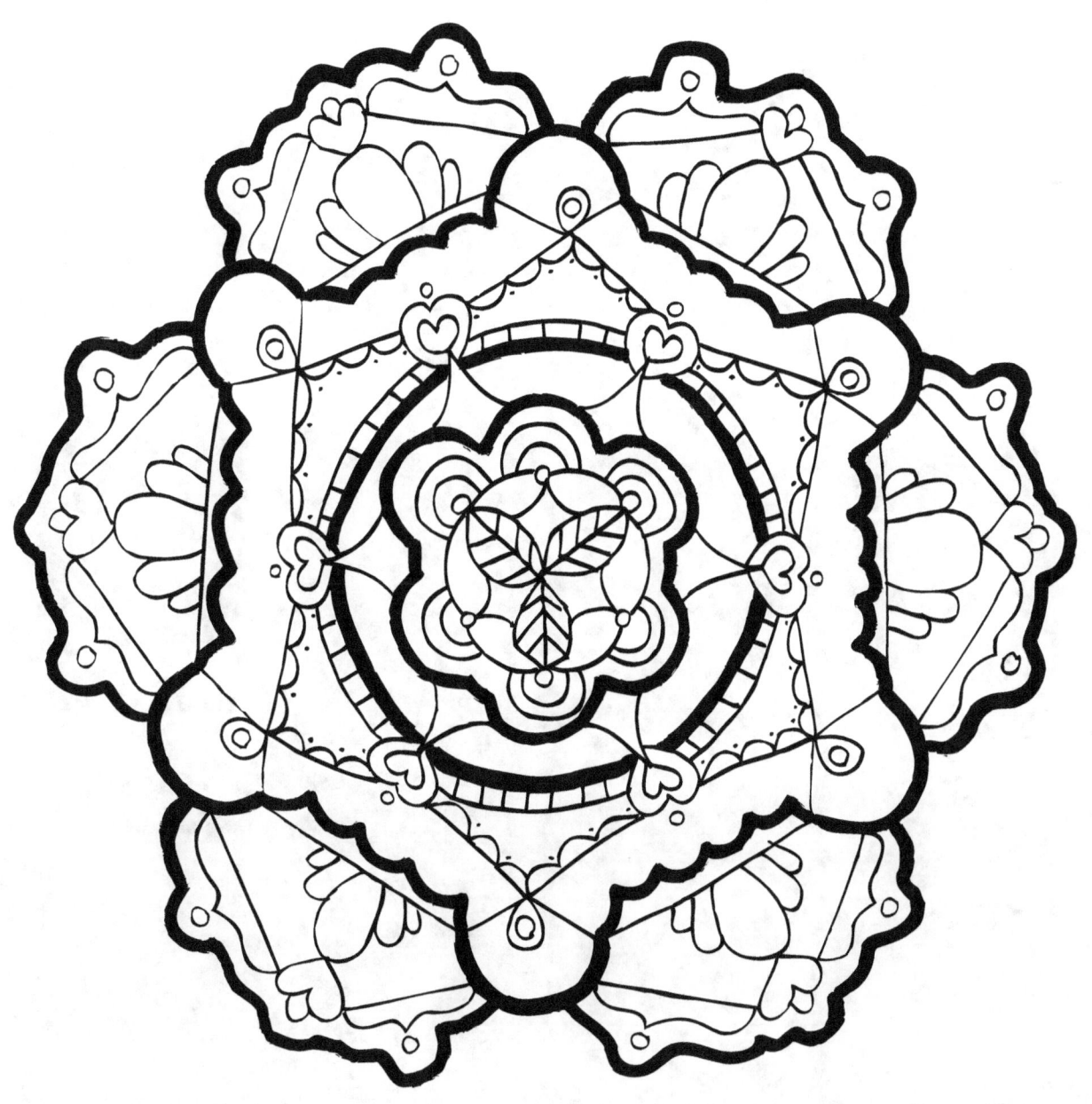

I am energetic, ambitious, and driven.

Date:_____

Journal about it...

_____

_____

_____

_____

_____

_____

_____

_____

_____

_____

_____

_____

_____

_____

_____

_____

Strength

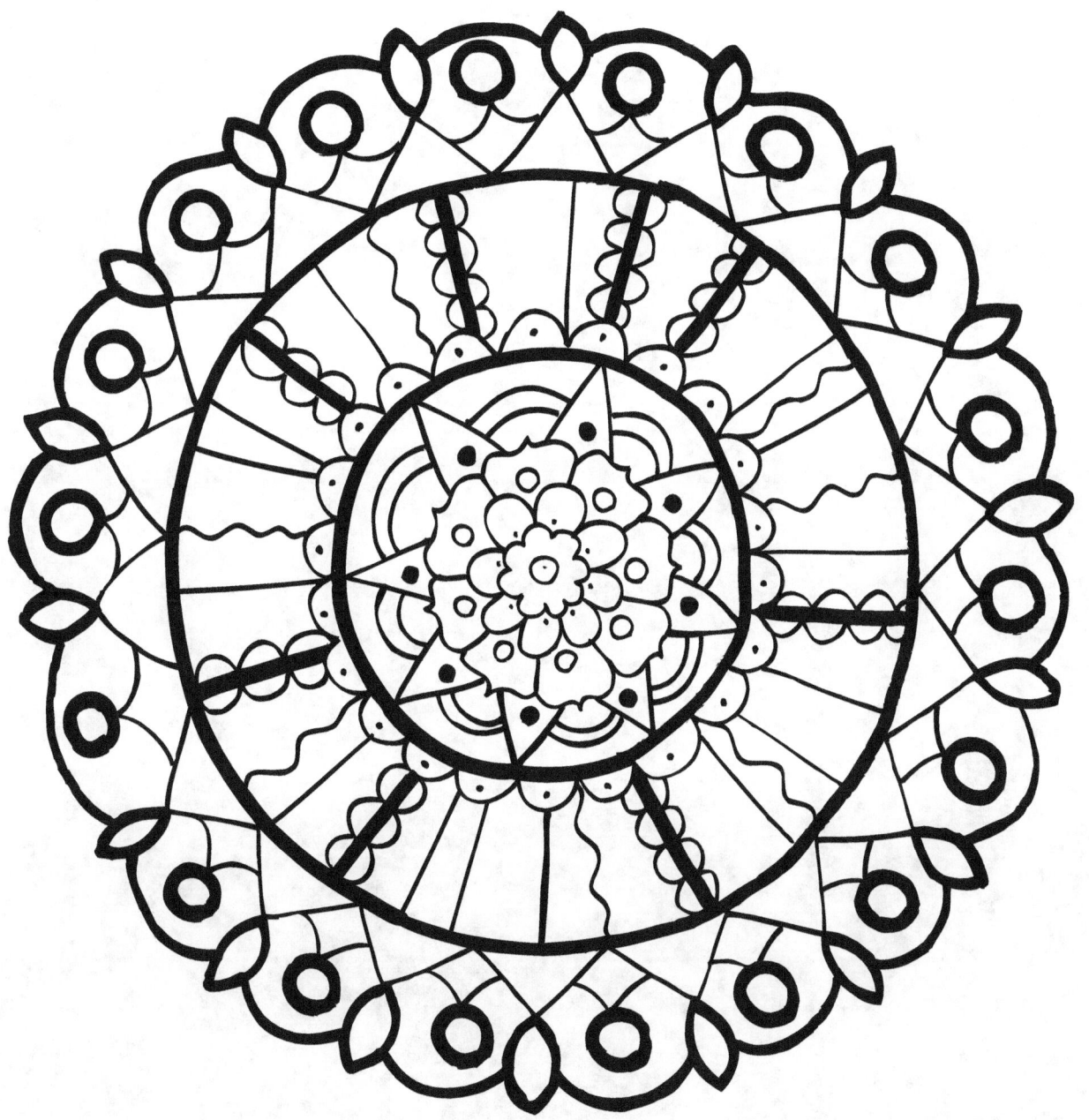

I have the courage to confront any challenges.

Date:_____

Journal about it...

_____

_____

_____

_____

_____

_____

_____

_____

_____

_____

_____

_____

_____

_____

_____

_____

_____

SPREAD THE DELICIOUS LOVE

*"We can't be so desperate for love that we
forget where we can always find it; within."*
- Alexandra Elle

The Heart Chakra is located at the center of the chest above the heart and is associated with the color green. This Chakra is the center of sympathy, empathy, and love. When you have a balanced Heart Chakra you have a sense of love and compassion to yourself and others. You will have feelings of self-acceptance and acceptance for others. If you have an overactive Heart Chakra, you may experience little control over your emotions. This may cause you to feel like you are constantly trying to please people and have a hard time receiving love from others. If you have an inactive or low active Chakra, you may experience depression and lack an ability to be caring or emote feelings of kindness. You may feel unworthy or unloved.

It is important to know about the Heart Chakra. We all have love for someone or something in our lives. Everyday stressors in life may cause us to forget about the things and people we love. Sometimes we are so busy that we forget to love ourselves. These negative feelings about yourself and others will absorb into your Heart Chakra causing this energy center to be blocked. It is important to balance your Heart Chakra in order to accept yourself and spread your love onto others.

The Heart Chakra is the fourth Chakra that needs to be addressed. I have been on both ends of the spectrum in having both low and high activity in my Heart Chakra. I have had difficulty in receiving love from others and also experienced feelings of being unloved. This goes back to the idea of being aware of how you feel about yourself. When you truly love yourself, you'll be able to spread that true love onto others.

I receive massages at least twice a month to balance my Heart Chakra. Being a massage therapist, I am constantly giving massages. In order for me to give a healing massage, I have to receive a healing massage for myself. I love to give myself that time to relax, because I know I deserve it. It feels great to be on the receiving end of a healing massage and meditate at the same time.

When I receive a massage, I focus on my Heart Chakra. Similar to meditating on my Root Chakra, I imagine a beam of light coming down onto the massage table and clear any unwanted energy and fill my heart with love. After my massage is over, I feel like my body is rejuvenated and it allows me to focus on what's important to me at that given moment in time.

I have massage clients who have told me after their session is over that they feel light and airy. I tell them that massage is a very healing experience, physically, mentally, and spiritually. It is a lot like meditation. Massage helps them forget about their hectic day, week, or month and allows them to focus on breath and relaxation.

If you receive more massages you will be able to balance your Heart Chakra along with the rest of your Chakras. You'll reach of a place of self-love, which will help you share your love with others. You may start to feel you can trust and forgive others, and in turn this may allow you to love yourself even more!

In the following coloring pages, pick a Mandala that you are attracted to at this moment. Complete this Mandala after getting a massage. If you are unable to receive a massage at the moment, close your eyes and meditate to your Heart Chakra. Focus on a bright white light at your heart and visualize this Chakra turning a beautiful bright green. As you color in your Mandala, continue to focus on your Heart Chakra. When you feel you have completed your Mandala, take time to journal about what you experienced before, during, and after coloring this particular Mandala.

Balance your Heart Chakra to feel self worth and accept all of those around you. By receiving massage, you will show yourself love and the ability to love those around you.

The Colorful Expressions of Your Soul by Crystal Simpelo

Value

I know and accept that I deserve love.

Date:_____

Journal about it...

_____

_____

_____

_____

_____

_____

_____

_____

_____

_____

_____

_____

_____

_____

_____

_____

_____

Love

I love and accept
myself unconditionally.

Date:_____

Journal about it...

_____

_____

_____

_____

_____

_____

_____

_____

_____

_____

_____

_____

_____

_____

_____

_____

_____

_____

Embrace

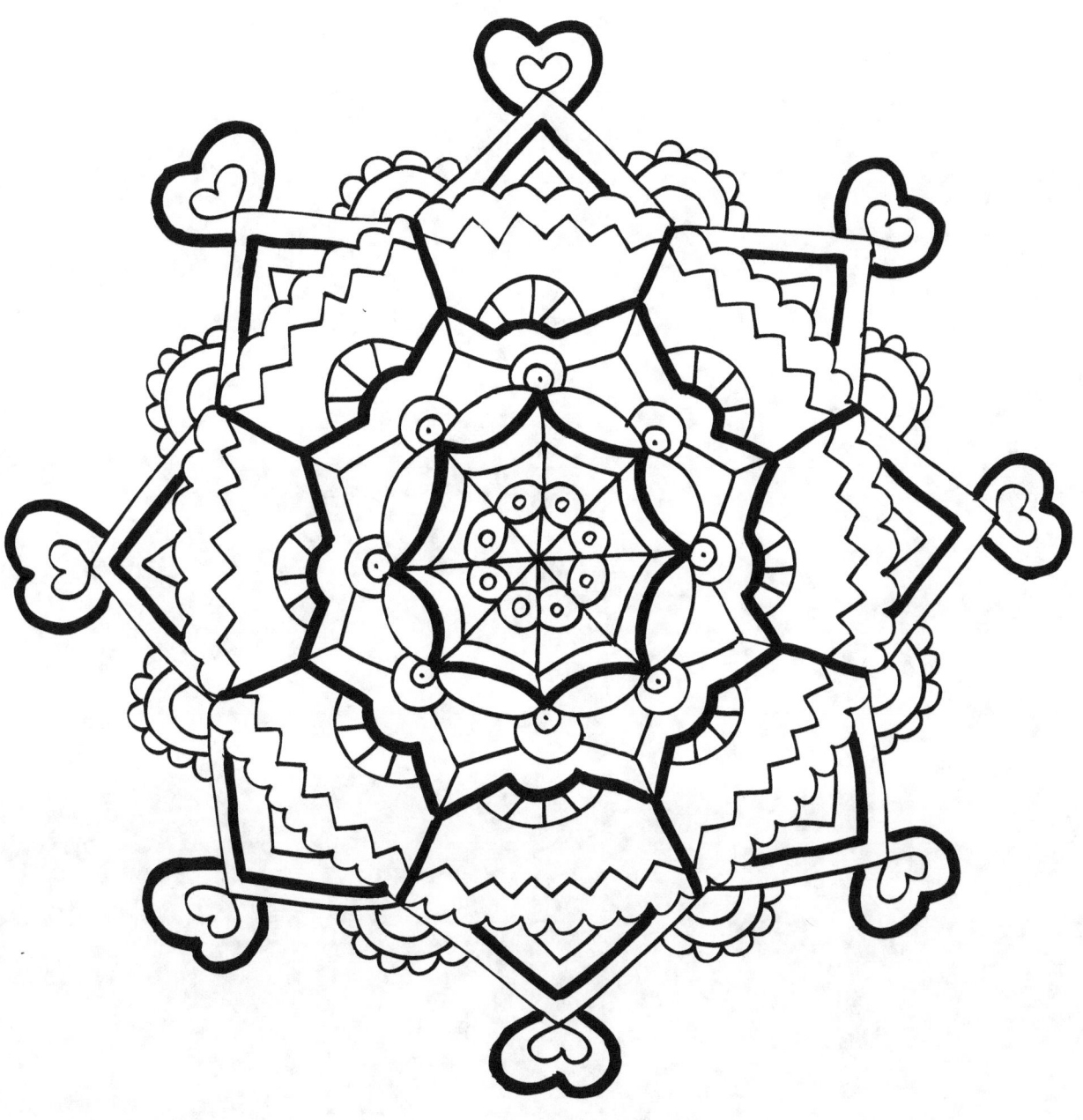

I open my heart to radiate love.

Date:_____

Journal about it...

_____

_____

_____

_____

_____

_____

_____

_____

_____

_____

_____

_____

_____

_____

_____

_____

_____

_____

_____

SING IT LIKE A ROCK STAR

"If everyone started off the day singing,
just think how happy they'd be."
- Lauren Myracle

The Throat Chakra is located at the throat and is associated with the color blue. This Chakra is the center of truth, communication, and self-expression. When you have a balanced Throat Chakra you have inner trust and the ability to express yourself freely. If you have an overactive Throat Chakra you may feel overly critical of others and might even have verbally abusive tendencies at times. If you have an inactive or low active Throat Chakra, you may have difficulty expressing yourself and telling the truth. You may feel like you are misunderstood and feel rejected.

It is important to know about the Throat Chakra. Communication can be difficult, especially when fear settles in. The negativity from the fear of nervousness when speaking in public or the fear of rejection when you don't know the outcome of a risk will absorb into your Throat Chakra causing this energy center to be blocked. It is important to balance your Throat Chakra in order to communicate your inner truth and express yourself freely.

The Throat Chakra is the fifth Chakra that needs to be addressed. As long as I could remember I have always had trouble speaking my mind and have been afraid of the future. From speech class to my artwork, there is the commonality of the fear and discomfort of the unknown outcome. If you just trust yourself, you will have the ability to express yourself in positive ways. Clearing this Chakra will allow you to understand and express your inner truth.

I sing to balance my Throat Chakra. Given I don't sing very well, but I sing! I usually find myself singing at the top of my lungs when I am driving or in the privacy of my own home. I also enjoy singing along with friends during karaoke at a local pizza joint, which we go to religiously. I turn up some of my favorite tunes and sing even when I do not know the words, because it makes me feel like a rock star. I no longer have a fear or care about the judgment or outcome, because I have nothing to lose and it makes me happy.

When I sing, I focus on my Throat Chakra. I have a variety of songs and artists that I listen to when I am feeling angry or sad. These are my "go to" songs. I associate these songs with feelings of love, peace, and happiness. When I sing these songs, I feel an almost instantaneous change in mood and thought. I am also able to take lyrics from these songs as signs for clarity and guidance. Something as simple as one word from a lyric can resonate in me, and it can have a huge impact on the way I feel for the rest of the day. Paying attention to what you are singing and taking what you want from lyrics is a great way to balance your Throat Chakra.

A singer can perform in front of an audience and feel comfortable and happy. They set stage fright aside and let their voice and/or instrument guide them into making beautiful music for others to enjoy, while enjoying the process themselves.

If you decide to use singing as a tool to balance your Throat Chakra, you may notice that you will gain positive and creative self-expression. You may be able to communicate your inner truth to others as well.

In the following coloring pages, pick a Mandala that you are attracted to at this moment. Complete this Mandala by listening to your favorite "go-to" song(s) and sing them outloud. Close your eyes and visualize yourself in front of a huge audience. Visualize yourself looking beautiful on stage and the audience clapping and cheering you on as you sing. Focus on a bright white light at your throat and visualize this Chakra turning to a beautiful bright blue. As you color in your Mandala, continue to focus on your Throat Chakra. When you feel you have completed your Mandala take time to journal about what you experienced before, during, and after coloring this particular Mandala.

Balance your Throat Chakra to allow your inner truth to come out, and have positive self-expression by visualizing yourself singing like a rock star in front of a cheering audience.

Dream

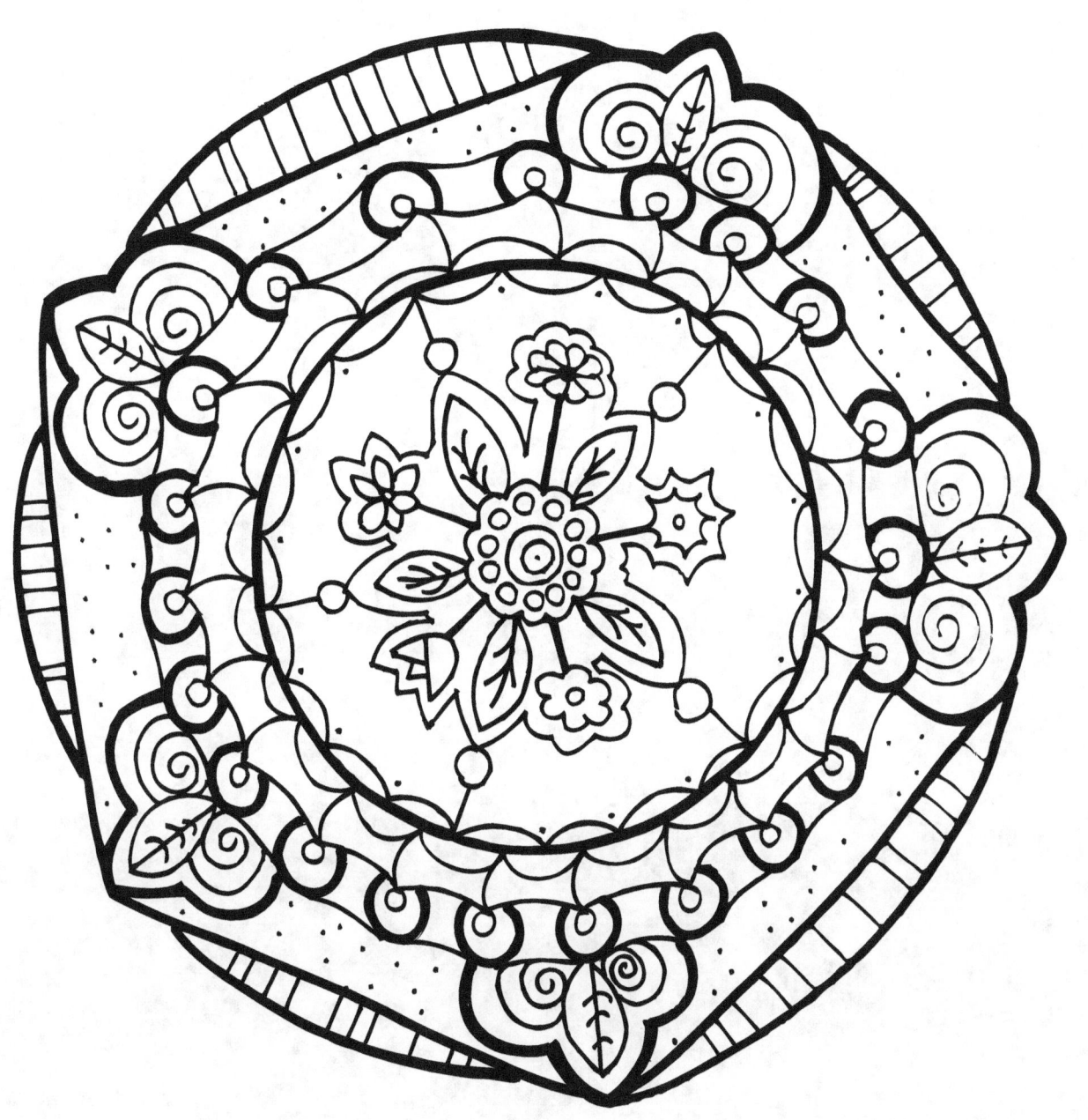

My dreams are filled
with positive guidance.

Date:_____

Journal about it...

_____

_____

_____

_____

_____

_____

_____

_____

_____

_____

_____

_____

_____

_____

_____

_____

Truth

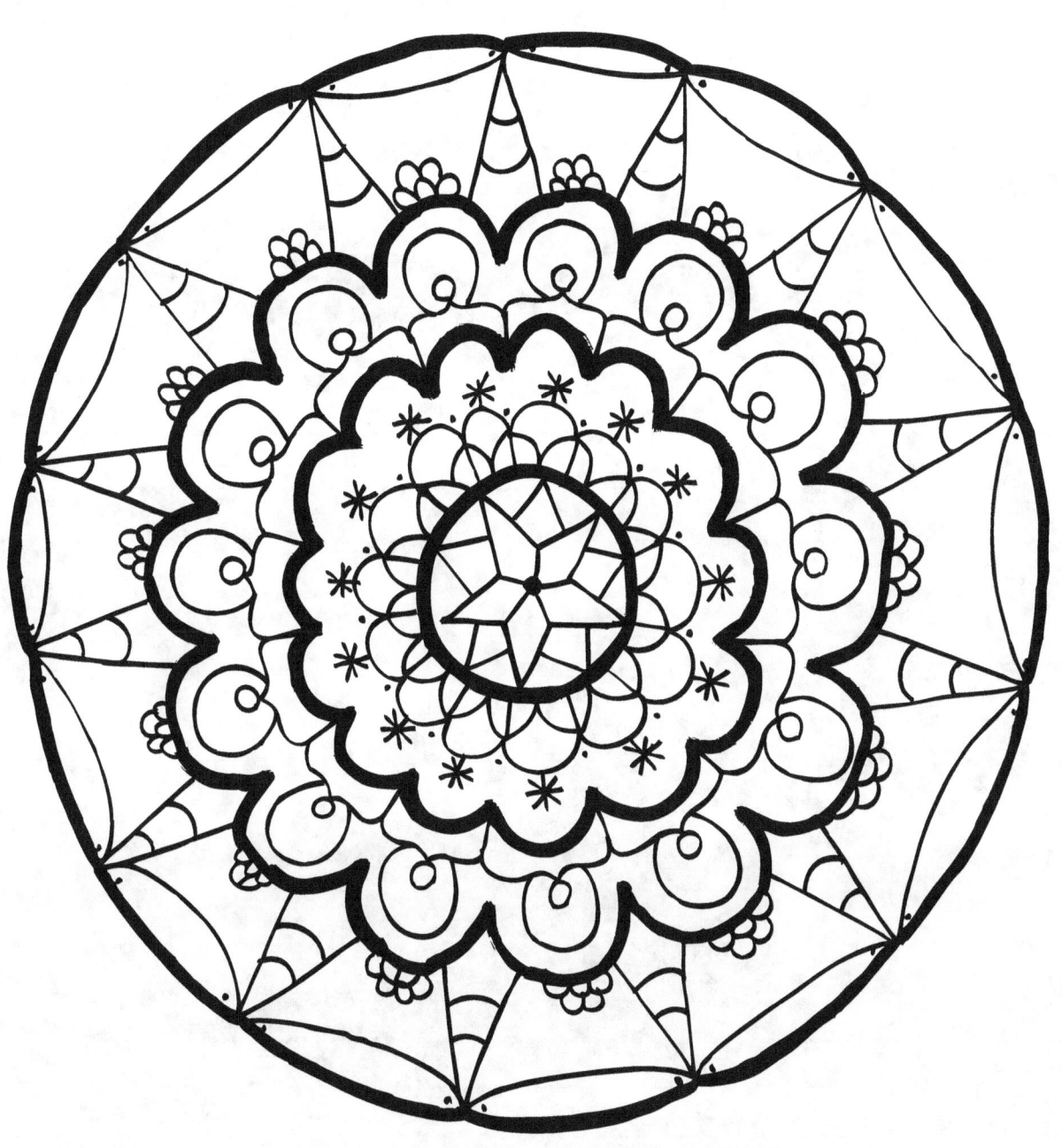

I speak easily and truthfully
to myself and others.

Date:_____

Journal about it...

_____

_____

_____

_____

_____

_____

_____

_____

_____

_____

_____

_____

_____

_____

_____

_____

_____

Communication

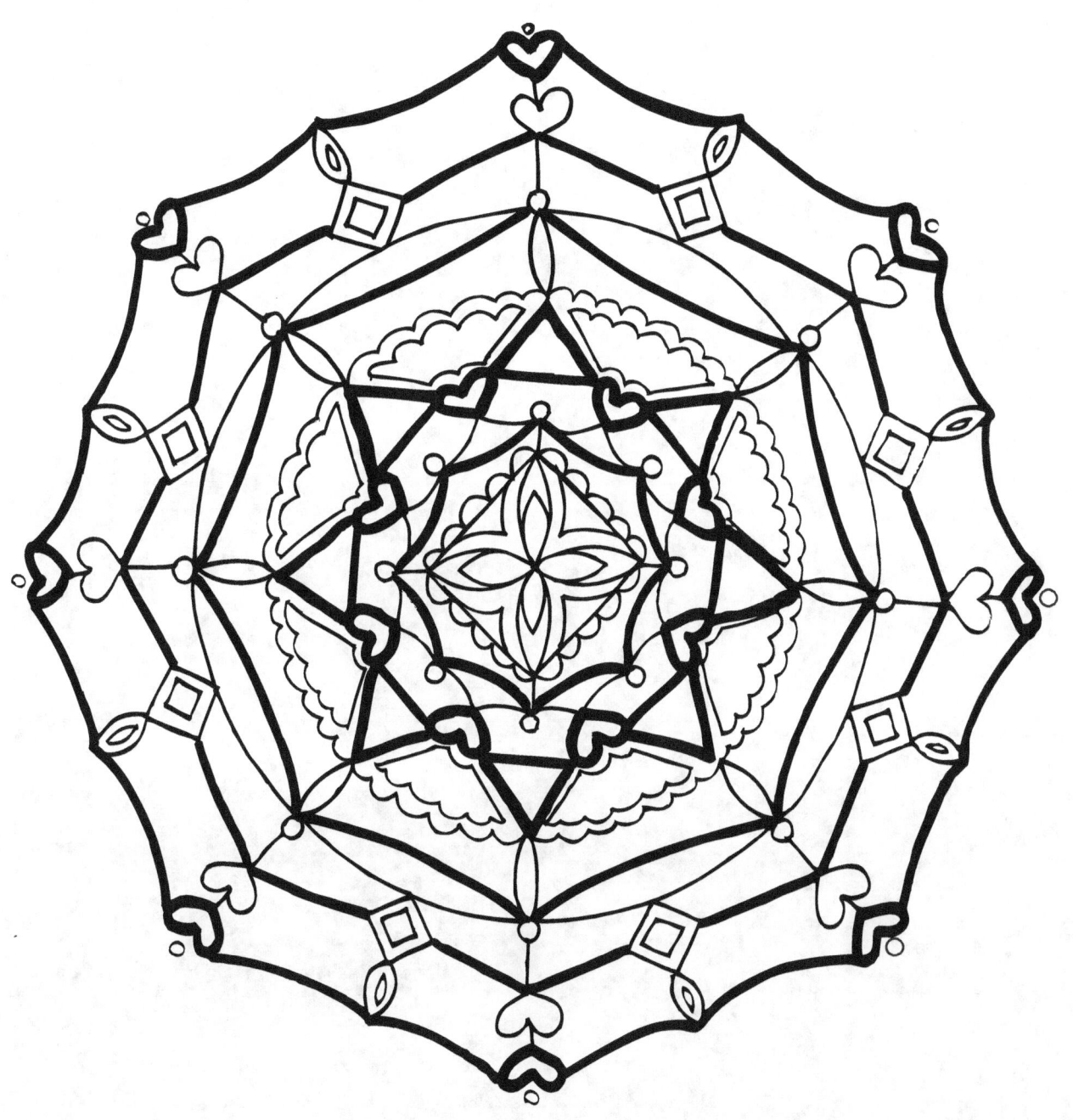

I am a confident speaker.

Date:_____

Journal about it...

_____

_____

_____

_____

_____

_____

_____

_____

_____

_____

_____

_____

_____

_____

_____

_____

_____

DO YOUR CRAZY DANCE

"There are short-cuts to happiness, and dancing is one of them."
- Vicki Baum

The Third Eye Chakra is located at our forehead in between the eyebrows and is associated with the color Indigo. This Chakra is the center of intuition, imagination, and perception. When you have a balanced Third Eye Chakra, you have a connection to yourself which results in a strong intuition. You have the knowledge, understanding, and focus in seeing the big picture. If you have an overactive Third Eye Chakra you may overthink things and have feelings of mental overload and confusion. If you have low activity or an inactive Third Eye Chakra you may feel mental blocks, lack spiritual connection, and lack imagination.

It is important to know about the Third Eye Chakra. Many times we find ourselves focusing on the bad things that take place. When we start off our day on a bad note, we sometimes dwell on the negative events that occurred throughout the rest of the day. This will attract other bad things to occur. These negative perceptions will absorb into your Third Eye Chakra, causing this energy center to be blocked. I believe that by making a conscious effort to change our thoughts in a positive way will attract goodness and positivity. It is important to balance your Third Eye Chakra in order to connect with all that is good and to have an understanding and focus of your big picture.

The Third Eye Chakra is the sixth Chakra that needs to be addressed. I used to wake up for work thinking of all the things I had to accomplish that day. I felt nervous and mentally exhausted even before I got out of bed! Losing control of my thoughts took a toll on me physically and mentally. Clearing your Third Eye Chakra will allow you to have a mental focus on seeing the big picture under a positive lens.

I dance to balance my Third Eye Chakra. Anyone that knows me knows that I love to dance. If one my favorite songs are on, I don't care what is happening I will be dancing until the song comes to an end. By doing so, I forget about my hectic day. Feeling the beat of the song and pondering what goofy dance move I am going to come up with next, gives me a sense of humor and relief.

When I dance, I feel free. When I am feeling frustrated about something, I can take a break, set my problems aside, and just dance. I imagine myself dancing happily with all my friends and family. One of my most memorable memories was dancing on my wedding day. I visualize myself dancing in the center of the dance floor with all the people I love, even those who have passed away or I have never met before. I imagine everyone smiling and dancing in their own way; pure joy, no judgment.

I know others who also love to dance. Whether it is a night out in the city, at a wedding, or in the privacy of their home, it is usually done when we feel good. Professional dancer or not, dancing puts us all in an uplifting and happy mood.

If you decide to use dance as a way to balance your Third Eye Chakra, you may feel like you can think clearly and focus better. You may feel like you have a free imagination.

In the following coloring pages pick a Mandala that you are attracted to at this moment. Complete this Mandala by dancing to your favorite song all the way through. Close your eyes, and visualize yourself dancing with your loving family and friends. Visualize yourself on *Soul Train* and each person has a chance to show what they have got. When it is your turn to dance, everyone is dancing along with you and cheering you on. Focus on a bright white light in between your eyebrows and visualize this Chakra turning a beautiful bright indigo. As you color in your Mandala, continue to focus on your Third Eye Chakra. When you feel that you have completed your Mandala, take time to journal about what you experienced before, during, and after coloring this particular Mandala.

Balance your Third Eye Chakra and allow yourself to free your imagination by dancing your heart out and visualize yourself taking part in a *Soul Train* line with your closest friends.

The Colorful Expressions of Your Soul by Crystal Simpelo

Imagine

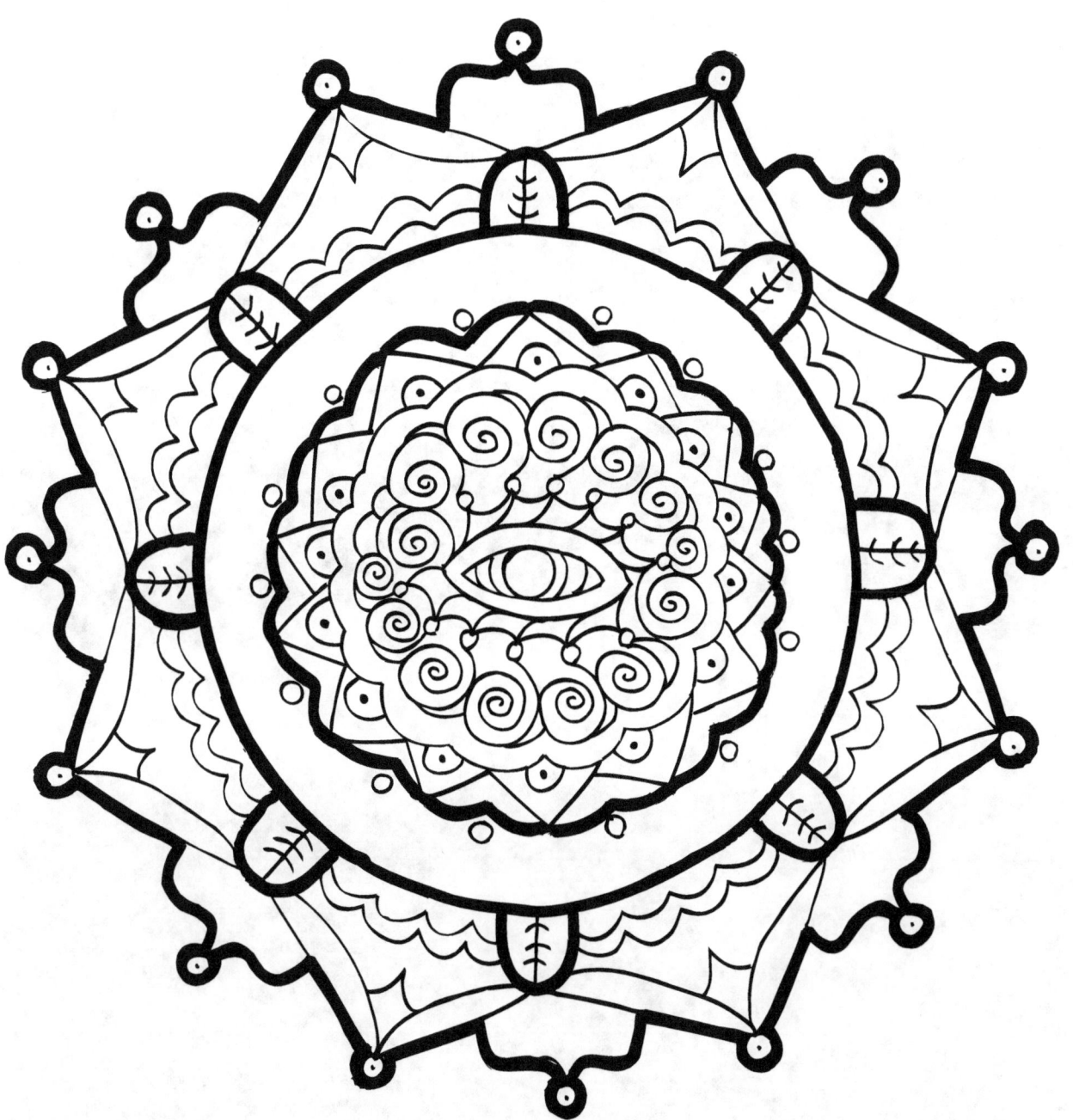

I use my imagination for
positive and creative purposes.

Date:_____

Journal about it...

_____

_____

_____

_____

_____

_____

_____

_____

_____

_____

_____

_____

_____

_____

_____

_____

_____

Smile

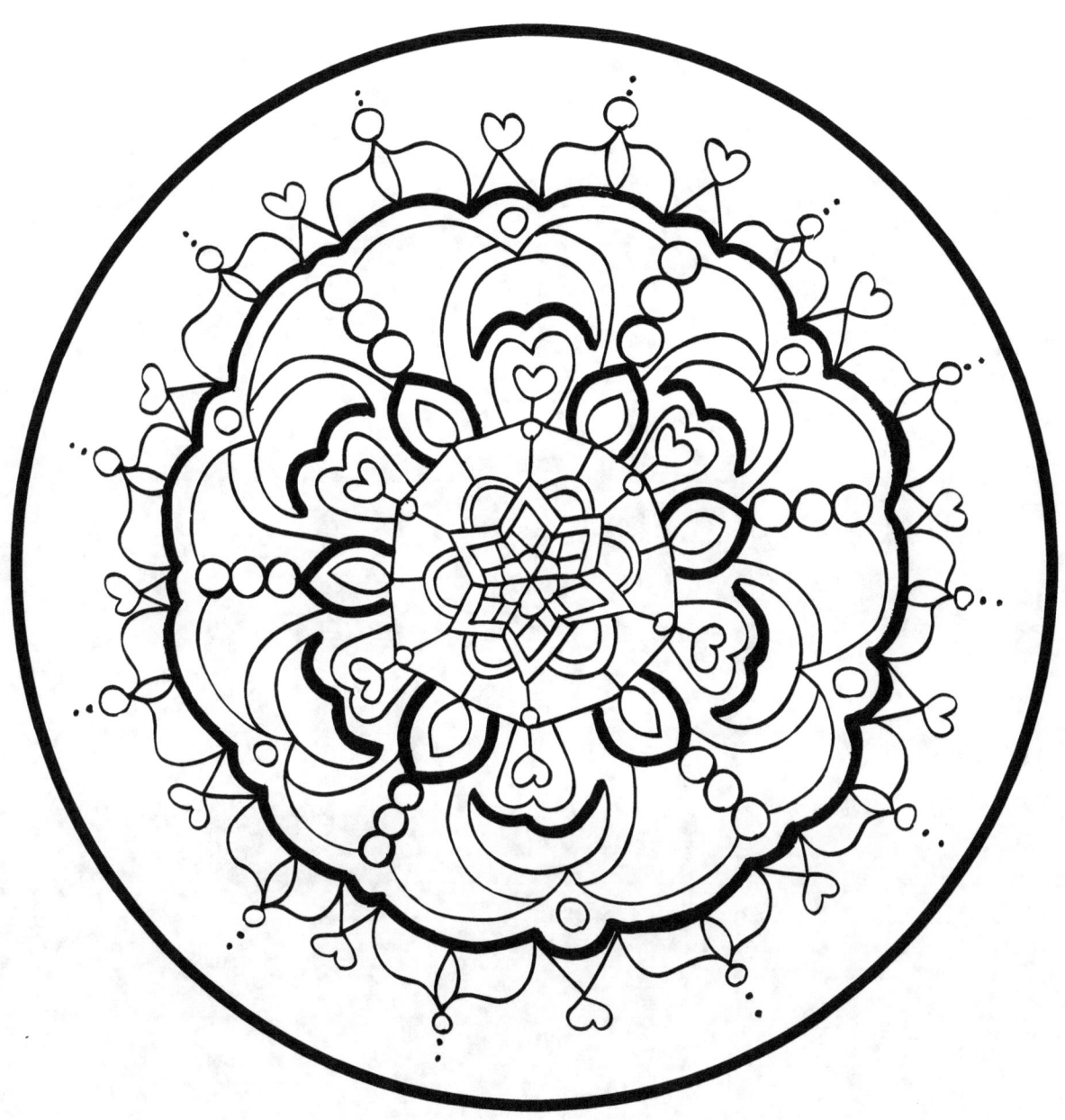

My happiness continues to
bring me more happiness.

Date:_____

Journal about it...

_____

_____

_____

_____

_____

_____

_____

_____

_____

_____

_____

_____

_____

_____

_____

_____

_____

_____

Dance

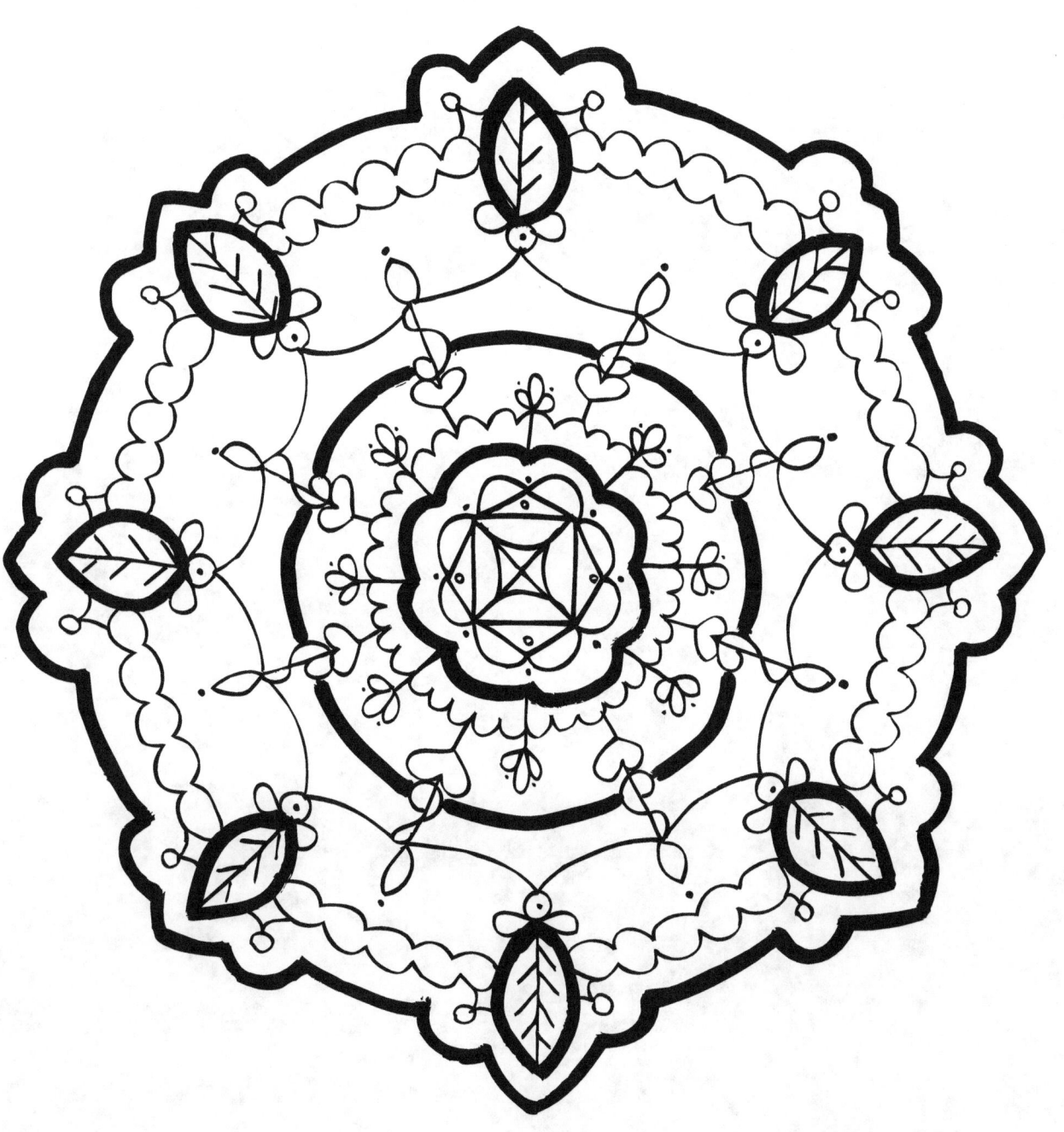

My life is filled with joy and laughter.

Date:_____

Journal about it...

_____

_____

_____

_____

_____

_____

_____

_____

_____

_____

_____

_____

_____

_____

_____

_____

_____

_____

_____

ARE YOU EVEN LISTENING?

"Affirmations are our mental vitamins,
providing the supplementary positive thoughts we need to balance the
barrage of negative events and thoughts we experience daily."
- Tia Walker

The Crown Chakra is located at the top of the head and is associated with the color violet. This Chakra is the center of creating connections and enlightenment with your higher self. When you have a balanced Crown Chakra, you are intuitive, aware, strong, and joyous. You are aware of yourself and see the well-being of others as a whole. If you have an overactive Crown Chakra you may over intellectualize, experience confusion, and have trouble grounding yourself. If you have low activity in your Crown Chakra, you may lack a connection to the universe and feel a lack of purpose in your own life. You may also lack desire to discover your inner self. Both of these are obviously not good outcomes. You must search for balance.

It is important to know about the Crown Chakra. You may question your career plan in life or have difficulties discovering your purpose in life. Knowing who you are and what you are capable of doing in life may unnecessarily appear to be stressful, and farfetched. These stressors will absorb into your Crown Chakra causing this energy center to be blocked. It is important to balance your Crown Chakra in order to see yourself freely connect with the universe and also see the well-being of others as a whole.

The Crown Chakra is the seventh and final Chakra that needs to be addressed. After all your Chakras have been balanced, this is the last one to be unblocked in order to reach awareness of your well-being and the well-being of others. Before creating this book I dealt with a blocked crown Chakra. This caused me to question my purpose in life and lack knowledge on what I was capable of doing with my time and energy. Clearing your Crown Chakra will allow you find your purpose and freely connect with the universe.

My solution to balance my Crown Chakra is to practice using positive affirmations every day. We all have days where we might feel sad, defeated, or angry. We can change these feelings by transforming our thoughts. We have the power. Instead of feeling sad or angry, we should redirect our energies into saying: "I am happy and at peace."

Saying: "I cannot help the way I feel" is a poor excuse and untrue. I was guilty of doing this myself, but boy was I wrong! I have learned so much in the past couple years about using positive affirmations. One instance in my life that stands out is when I started working with my business mentor. At the time I was not attracting enough massage clients to make ends meet. My mentor first introduced me to the use of positive affirmations. This is what we came up with: "I am a successful massage therapist, and I have twenty clients per week and attract abundance in money with ease and grace." This seemed foolish to me, because I couldn't possibly help the fact that I was not getting clients. Regardless, I listened to my mentor and wrote my affirmation on post-its and stuck them everywhere I knew I would see them, such as my computer screen and on my bathroom mirror. Within the next couple months, I was seeing an increase in my client base per week, and was bringing in more money!

I know some of my fellow massage therapists have implemented the solution of positive affirmations in building their massage business. They are able to attract the right clientele to make referral clients and more money. Win, win!

If you decide to practice using positive affirmations in your life to balance your Crown Chakra, you will start to feel a spiritual connection and have better intuition. You will start to have a better connection to the universe.

In the following coloring pages pick a Mandala that seems attractive to you at this given moment. Complete this Mandala by writing down or thinking about a positive affirmation. When coming up with your positive affirmations, remember to be specific in what you want. Use words in the present tense. Start them off with "I am" or "I feel," and stay away from phrases that start with "I will" or "I hope." Close your eyes and visualize

The Colorful Expressions of Your Soul by Crystal Simpelo

yourself living this positive affirmation. Focus on a bright white light at the top of your head and visualize this Chakra turning a beautiful bright violet. As you color in your Mandala, continue to focus on your Crown Chakra. When you feel you have completed your Mandala take time to journal about what you experienced before, during, and after coloring this particular Mandala.

Balance your Crown Chakra by practicing and believing your positive affirmations to feel one with the universe.

The Colorful Expressions of Your Soul by Crystal Simpelo

Enlightenment

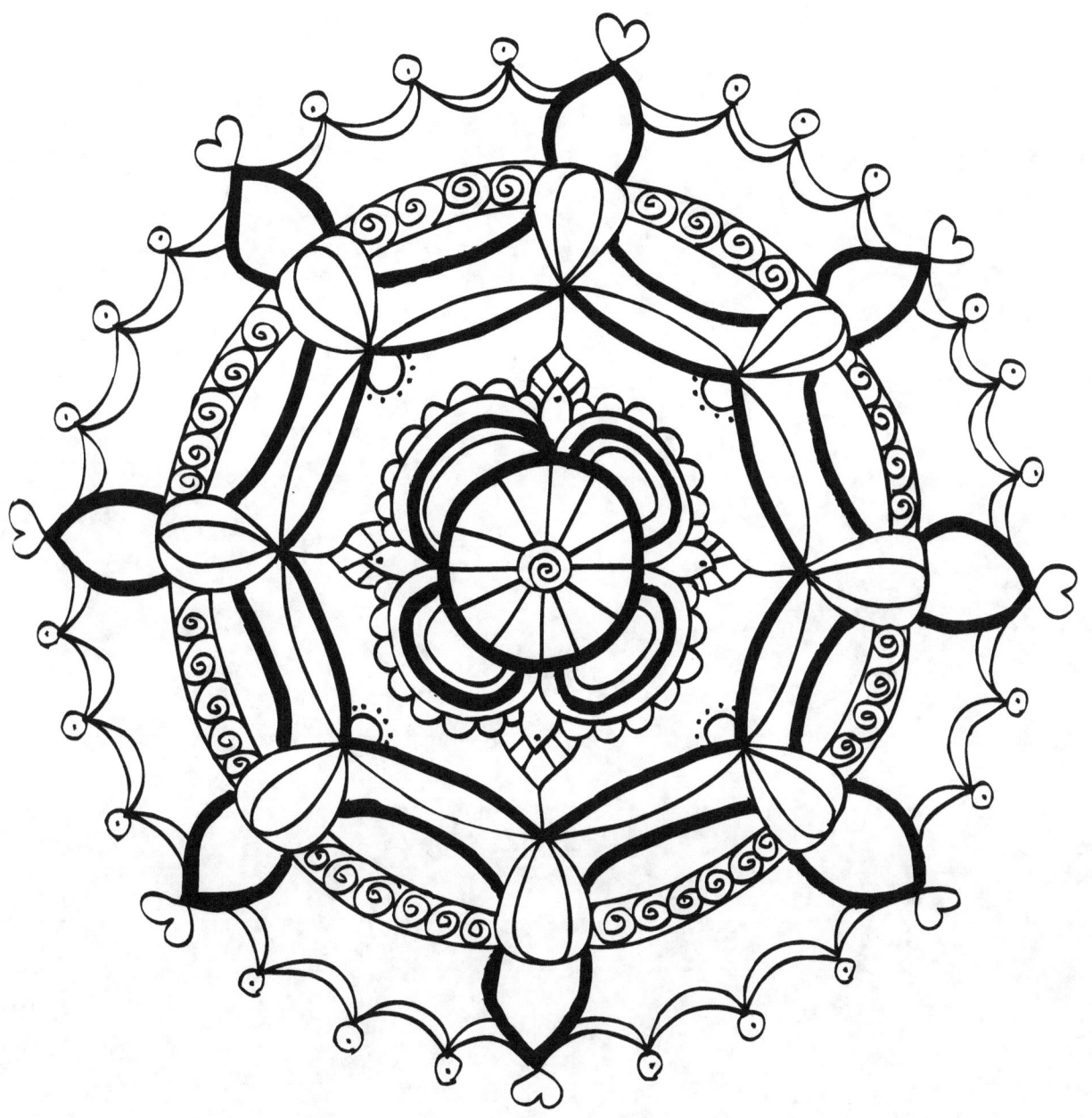

I have full control of my
thoughts and emotions.

Date:_____

Journal about it...

_____

_____

_____

_____

_____

_____

_____

_____

_____

_____

_____

_____

_____

_____

_____

_____

_____

_____

_____

Awakening

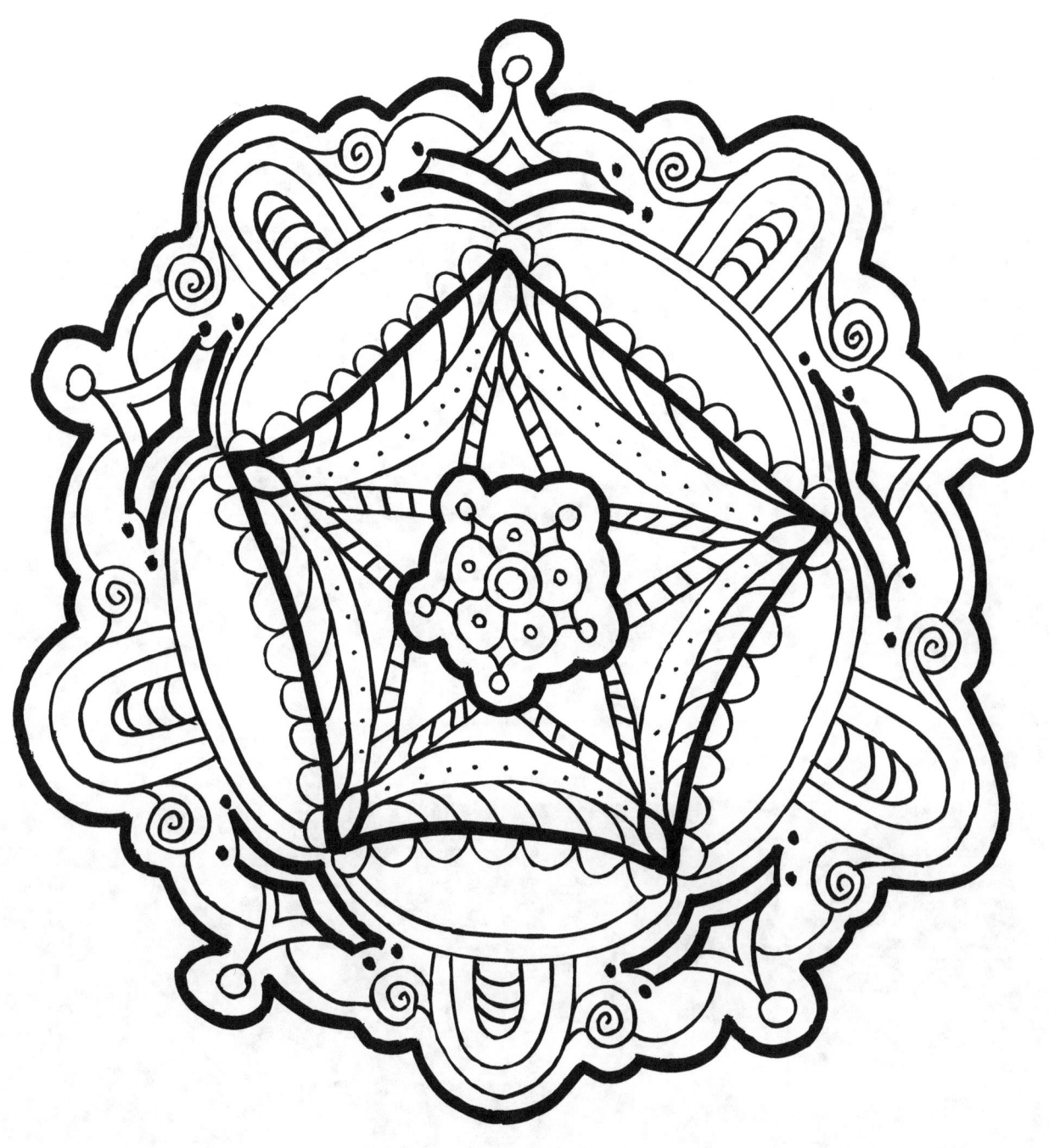

I am fully present in everything that I do.

Date: _____

Journal about it...

_____
_____
_____
_____
_____
_____
_____
_____
_____
_____
_____
_____
_____
_____
_____
_____
_____
_____
_____

Intuition

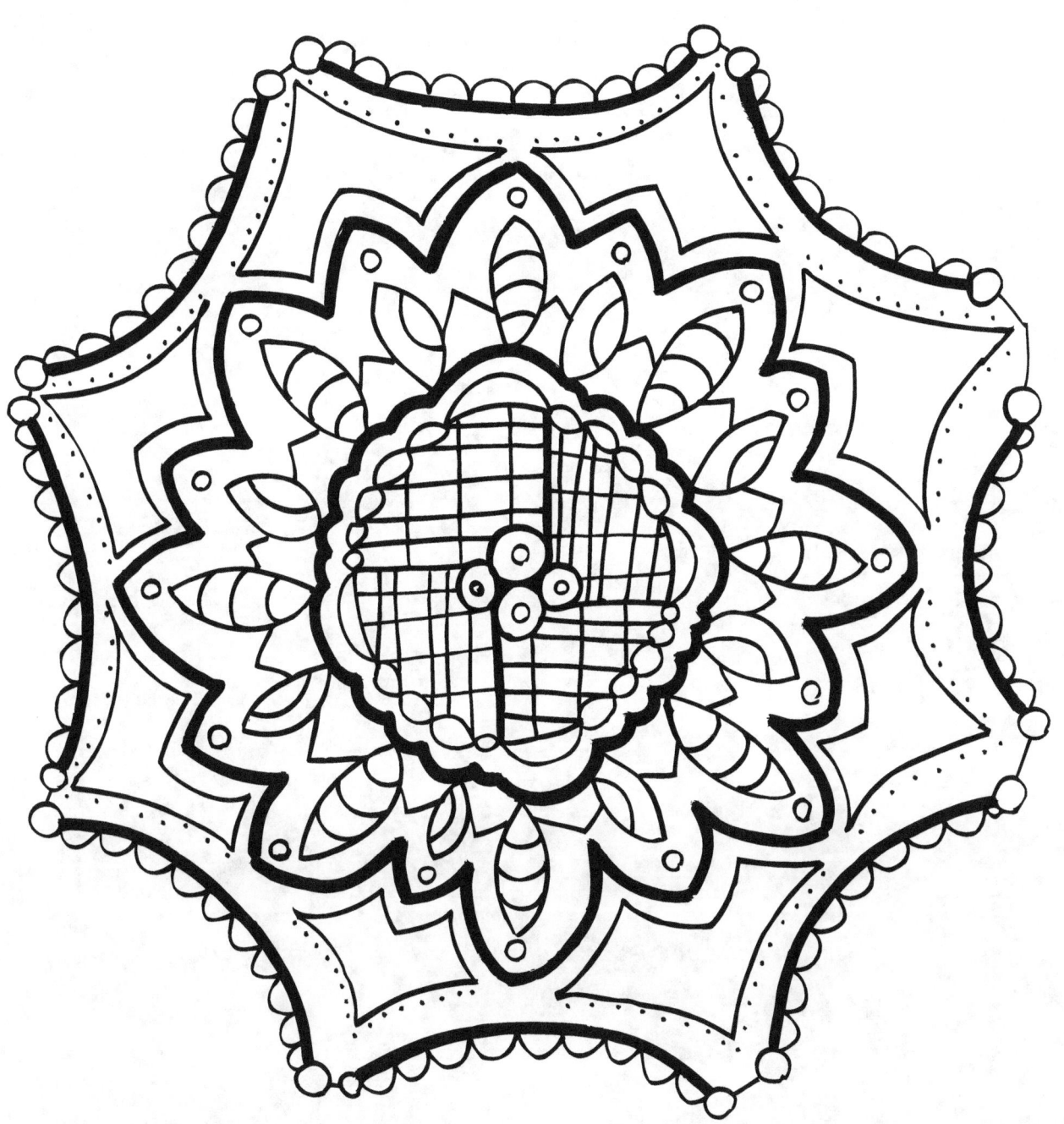

I always listen to my intuition
and find the perfect answers.

Date:_____

Journal about it...

_____

_____

_____

_____

_____

_____

_____

_____

_____

_____

_____

_____

_____

_____

_____

_____

_____

_____

TIME TO EMBARK ON YOUR JOURNEY

"The world is a book, and those who don't travel read only one page." –Augustine of Hippo

Congratulations on reading my book and applying these fun meditative art tools to implement into your life. Thank you for taking the time to learn my tools for balancing your chakras while incorporating my love of art.

I know that you have finished reading my book, but this is not the end, my friend! You now have mirrored images of your inner-self that you have created! That is pretty awesome, but now what you have to do is go back and meditate to your creations and read your journal entries to remind yourself of how amazing you felt after coloring each one.

If you are having a horrible day or are feeling like you have been stuck in a funk, then close your eyes and pick a random page from your coloring book. Read your journal entry and then meditate to that Mandala to gain some peace of mind and maybe even find answers to things you have been questioning.

Meditative art has been a constant in my life since I was a little girl. I may not have known it at the time, but creating art has always quieted my mind and allowed me to focus on whatever it was that I needed to. Art makes me joyful. I was able to take my art to a new level and allowed it to be my personal tool for Chakra balancing meditation. Implementing these visualizations and drawing these Mandalas has changed my life tremendously, and I am so excited to have shared them with you, so you can embark on the same journey I did!

I hope you realize that by implementing meditative art into your life can change yourself in countless positive ways. Be creative and feel the positive vibes within; everything will fall into place. Feel your chakras balance. Let yourself shine. Release your inner child. Be one with nature. Take care of yourself. Sing like a rock star. Dance your heart out. Practice positive affirmations constantly. By doing all of these things, you have the power to heal yourself physically, emotionally, and spiritually! Be excited to feel grounded, creative, confident, and loving. Be ready to have a positive self-expression, a great intuition, and a joy for life. Positive changes are happening now and will continue to happen in your future. I hope you have fallen in love with art.

I love knowing that these fun tools had such a positive impact on my life. I felt called to share my love for meditative art with you so you can feel the same way. Simply knowing that others can benefit from visualizing and coloring my Mandalas is such an awesome feeling, and doing so with you, is even more so.

Now it's up to you; go make the world a better place! Continue using these tools you have learned and share the love with others. After all, "the Earth without 'art' is just 'eh.'"

FREQUENTLY ASKED QUESTIONS

How can I cut the Mandalas out from this book?

First, place a piece of thick cardboard or foam board underneath the page you would like to cut out. Then, use a ruler and X-acto knife or blade to cut the top of the page. You can cut and frame your mandala in an 8x10 frame or display them in your place of choice.

What does a balanced Root Chakra feel like and how do I balance it?

When you have a balanced Root Chakra, you may experience feelings of security, financial independence, balance, and stability. Ground your Root Chakra by visualizing it shining as bright as the sun; then you will feel committed, strong, grounded, and energetic.

What does a balanced Sacral Chakra feel like and how do I balance it?

When you have a balanced Sacral Chakra, you may experience free flowing creativity and engage in passionate relationships. Balance your Sacral Chakra by releasing your inner-child and be creative with others to attract healthy relationships.

What does a balanced Solar Plexus Chakra feel like and how do I balance it?

When you have a balanced Solar Plexus Chakra, you may have self-confidence, achieve your goals, and gain a strong sense of motivation towards your desires. Balance your Solar Plexus Chakra by visualizing yourself at your happy place in nature to feel strong, confident, and energetic.

What does a balanced Heart Chakra feel like and how do I balance it?

When you have a balanced Heart Chakra, you may gain a sense of love and compassion. You may have feelings of self-acceptance and understand and accept others as well. Balance your Heart Chakra to reach a sense of self-worth and have acceptance of others by receiving massages to show love towards yourself.

What does a balanced Throat Chakra feel like and how do I balance it?

When you have a balanced Throat Chakra, you may experience inner trust and the ability to express yourself freely. Balance your Throat Chakra in order to allow your inner truth to come out. You can use positive self-expression by visualizing yourself singing like a rock star on stage in front of a cheering audience.

What does a balanced Third Eye Chakra feel like and how do I balance it?

When you have a balanced Third Eye Chakra, you may have a connection to yourself and reach a strong intuition. You may have the knowledge, understanding, and focus in seeing your big picture. Balance your Third Eye Chakra and allow yourself to focus and free your imagination by dancing your heart out and visualize yourself taking part in a *Soul Train* line with your closest friends!

What does a balanced Crown Chakra feel like and how do I balance it?

When you have a balanced Crown Chakra, you may be intuitive, aware, strong, and joyous. You may be more aware of yourself and start to notice the well-being of others as a whole. Balance your Crown Chakra by practicing and believing your positive affirmations to feel one with the universe.

The Colorful Expressions of Your Soul by Crystal Simpelo

How do all these Chakras affect each other?

All of our chakras are working with one another. When any of your Chakras are imbalanced, it may cause others to be imbalanced as well. We want all of our Chakras to be in alignment with one another to experience a natural flow.

What is an effective way to balance your Chakras?

Practice using positive affirmations every day. We all have had days in which we've felt sad, defeated, or angry. We can change this feeling by simply gaining control over our thoughts. Instead of feeling sad or angry, simply transform it into "I am happy and at peace."

How do you know if your Chakras are imbalanced?

If we are not feeling good about ourselves, then it has a negative effect on our choices and clouds any sense of motivation towards what we desire. If we believe in what we are worth, then everything else will fall into place in a positive way.

FINAL THOUGHTS

Remember, this is not the end of the road. Continue to create and take what you want from the tools I've shared. You have and will gain transformation and personal growth in your life, physically, emotionally, and spiritually through the colorful expressions of your soul.

I would love to see your interpretations of the Mandalas in my book! Please post them to www.CrystalSimpelo.com or e-mail me at info@CrystalSimpelo.com. I would also love for you to share your stories/journal entries. Until then, keep creating!

ABOUT THE AUTHOR

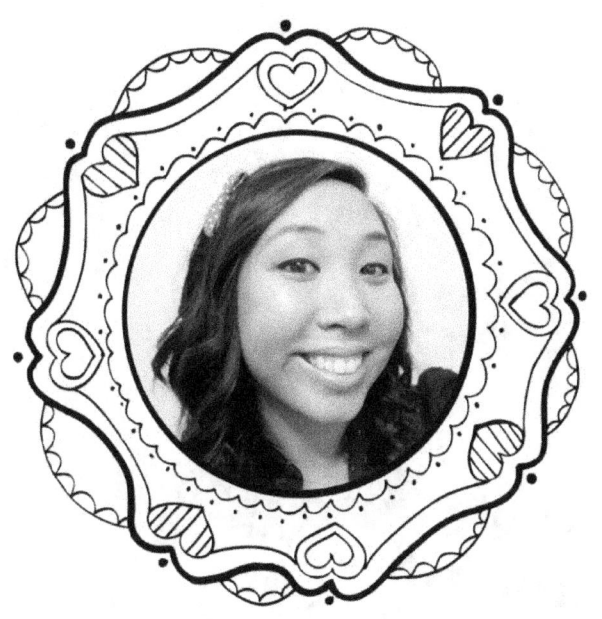

Crystal Simpelo is truly an artist at heart. From the day she was born, she was obsessed with coloring which eventually evolved into her love of learning new ways to use that art. As a kid, she also knew that she wanted to be a teacher. Now she currently facilitates "Heart to Art" workshops in the Chicagoland area, teaching people both art and meditation techniques, as she reminds her students the importance of the connection between heart and art. Simpelo's professional expertise as an artist was established when she obtained her Bachelor's Degree in Fine Arts from the Northern Illinois University with a concentration on Interactive Art. Her creative nature is also extended into her Massage Therapy practice, where clients have raved about her as "THE best massage therapist and overall healer in the Chicagoland area." Simpelo currently lives in her hometown of Lombard, IL with her loving husband. When she's not creating art from the heart, you can find her playing the piano, checking out live music, and hanging out with her friends. Simpelo's mission in life is to raise the vibration of this world and promote a positive state of being through art.

Visit CrystalSimpelo.com today to learn more!

The Colorful Expressions of Your Soul by Crystal Simpelo

FREE CHAKRA POSTER!

Would you like a visual representation of where the seven main Chakras are located on your body? Of course you do!

That's why I'm giving away copies of a beautiful Chakra poster that I hand-painted myself! I created this 8x10 painting using my favorite medium. Watercolors! In the painting I highlight where the seven Chakras are located and used a blend of all the colors of our Chakras to come together as one cohesive art piece. It's absolutely gorgeous and it's all yours for free!

Please visit **www.CrystalSimpelo.com** to download your free poster today!

Feel Free to print out multiple copies of the poster and display it in a frame or hang it on the fridge. You can even give away extra copies to family and friends. I hope that my painting will be a reminder for you to balance your Chakras on a regular basis, and live your life to the fullest!

www.ingramcontent.com/pod-product-compliance
Lightning Source LLC
Chambersburg PA
CBHW081729220526
45468CB00008B/2029